PROGRAMMING IN C

For the Microcomputer User

PROGRAMMING IN C

FOR THE MICROCOMPUTER USER

Robert J. Traister

Prentice-Hall, Inc., Englewood Cliffs, N.J. 07632

Library of Congress Cataloging in Publication Data

TRAISTER, ROBERT J. (date)
  Programming in C, for the microcomputer user.

  Includes index.
  1. C (Computer program language) I. Title.
QA76.73.C15T7 1984   001.64′24   83-17794
ISBN 0-13-729641-X

$$QA$$
$$76.73$$
$$.C15$$
$$T7$$
$$1984$$

ENGINEERING
& PHYSICS
LIBRARY

Editorial/production supervision
and interior design: **Karen Skrable**
Manufacturing buyer: **Anthony Caruso**
Cover design: **George Cornell**

© 1984 by **Prentice-Hall, Inc.**, Englewood Cliffs, N.J. 07632

Printed in the United States of America

10 9 8 7 6 5 4 3 2 1

ISBN 0-13-729641-X

Prentice-Hall International, Inc., *London*
Prentice-Hall of Australia Pty. Limited, *Sydney*
Editora Prentice-Hall do Brasil, Ltda., *Rio de Janeiro*
Prentice-Hall Canada Inc., *Toronto* '
Prentice-Hall of India Private Limited, *New Delhi*
Prentice-Hall of Japan, Inc., *Tokyo*
Prentice-Hall of Southeast Asia Pte. Ltd., *Singapore*
Whitehall Books Limited, *Wellington, New Zealand*

To
Carla and **Melvin Baugher**

CONTENTS

7 Going Further
With C *117*

PREFACE

If you're an average microcomputer user, then there's a very good chance that you have only recently heard of the C programming language, or simply C. There are several reasons for this, not the least of which is the fact that C was developed at Bell Laboratories in the last half of the previous decade. C, then, is a new language. Since its inception, its use has been relatively confined to the business world of minicomputers. Only recently has it begun to make inroads in microcomputers and among microcomputer operators.

As of this writing, many major software manufacturers are writing all their programs in C language. This does not mean that microcomputers will no longer be using BASIC, since these programs are compiled to run on microcomputers. Once the program developed by the software company has been compiled for a particular machine, it will run just as if it were written in BASIC, only much faster.

Of course, there are other languages that can be used for fast execution. So why are many companies switching to C? There are many reasons for this, but probably the major one is the straightforward nature of C. It is not bogged down with a great deal of complex structure. It's easy to use. One might even say that C is the BASIC language for system-level programming.

C was designed to optimize run time, size, and efficiency factors in almost any type of program. It was specifically designed to be machine independent. This means that a program written for one type of computer can be easily transferred to another machine with a minimum of modification. C is a programmer's language. It was designed by Dennis Ritchie at Bell Laboratories to make difficult programming jobs much easier.

While C was designed for professional programmers—as opposed to BASIC, which was designed for the average individual (supposedly)—one must remember the time which has elapsed since this all-purpose language was developed at Dartmouth College. This took place some 10 years prior to the development of C, and since that time, many "average" programmers have attained a much-higher level of programming proficiency on their home microcomputers than was ever anticipated.

C language does have many uses when coupled with today's personal computers. Each month, the differences between personal computers and minicomputers become less obvious. The same may be said to a lesser extent of the programmers who operate each type of machine.

If you have used BASIC for a few years, you have an excellent understanding of just what this language can accomplish. Moreover, you may understand even more about what cannot be accomplished or what is quite difficult to accomplish using BASIC. Of course, many, many persons who use microcomputers are accustomed only to the BASIC interpreter built into their machine. Many of them may have no idea whatsoever about the operation of compilers that can be used to allow these machines to operate under programs written in other languages, such as FORTRAN, Pascal, COBOL, and, more recently, C.

For this reason, this book begins with the absolute basics. If you have never used a compiler before, you will find an overview in the opening chapters that will guide you. An easily available, inexpensive compiler was used as a model for running programs presented in this book. Those available from other suppliers should present very few (if any) conversion difficulties when used in conjunction with information presented in this book.

It is to be hoped that as you read through the pages of this text, you will be reminded of your first few lessons in learning BASIC. The presentation of information is handled on about the same level. To further facilitate ease of understanding, the functions and statements found in C are referenced to BASIC statements and functions which you should already be familiar with. This is a new approach. You must remember that C was originally developed for the professional programmer, and thus most of the excellent instructional information available for this language is aimed at these individuals. This is not to say that the information cannot be very useful to the average microcomputer user, for it can. However, this can be a very difficult study and, as often as not, many people simply give up after reaching the first apparently insurmountable snag.

It is hoped that this text will serve as a primer to C language. It is designed to take you to a point in your education that will remove the cobwebs and gray areas that have hampered you from being able to use the standard reference manuals available.

One major failing of many tutorial texts dealing with any language is the printing and discussion of program segments rather than complete working programs. Nearly every program presented in this book is a working entity unto itself. Each may be input exactly as shown, compiled, and run on your machine. Some minor modifications may be necessary when dealing with other compilers, but in many instances, this will not be so.

If you can remember back to the days when you were studying BASIC for the first time, you will probably recall that any guides you read probably started with the basic PRINT statement and, after explaining it fully, proceeded onward to LET, INPUT, FOR-NEXT, and so on. The good ones taught by briefly defining a statement or function and then showing you exactly how each performs in a simple program. This is the format used throughout most of this book.

Undoubtedly, some system-level programmers who are quite familiar with C will throw up their hands in disgust at the sight of some of the simple program examples presented here. They might wonder why anyone in their right mind would write a dice game in a professional's language like C. This is nothing short of sacrilegious. However, if you think seriously about the programming aspects involved in presenting a fairly accurate game of craps, you must admit it's a pretty good exercise.

More to the point, this book is not aimed at the "professional" programmer, the one who is currently employed in a field that demands a high-level education in computer science, concepts, and languages. Rather, the information found here is directed toward the average person who has been writing serious programs in BASIC and wants to go further.

While it is difficult for any author to make specific guarantees, it is safe to say that if you have not programmed in C prior to reading this book, you will be programming in this beautifully simple language within a few hours. You will also gain an understanding of many of the functions, statements, and general formats used in C language, which you can reference directly to the language you are currently most familiar with, BASIC. When you have finished this study, you should be in a better position to make better use of the intermediate- and high-level materials that are available in this language. By absorbing all the information in this book, you will certainly *not* be in a position to call yourself a professional C programmer, but you will know how to program in this language, and it should be a fairly easy matter to progress further in efficiency. Just how far you progress is left up to you.

ROBERT J. TRAISTER

ACKNOWLEDGMENT

The author would like to acknowledge with gratitude the professional assistance provided by the programmers, staff, and management of Super-Soft, Inc. In addition to supplying the model C Language Compiler used in this text, this company's programmers also provided constant encouragement and expert information. Without their assistance, this work would not have been possible.

PROGRAMMING IN C

For the Microcomputer User

1 C PROGRAMMING LANGUAGE

2

3

4

5

6

7

What is C programming language? According to one of its developers, it is a general-purpose programming language that features economy of expression, modern control flow and data structures, and a rich set of operators. C is a high-level language, but among high-level languages, it is near the bottom as far as level is concerned. This low level relates to structure complexity and not to the actual usefulness of the language. The fact that C is written in a nonspecialized manner makes it more convenient for many programming tasks, especially those that may be targeted to a large variety of different microprocessors.

One cannot think of C language without also thinking of the UNIX operating system. It is for this high-level system that C language was originally designed. This operating system, the C compiler, and nearly all of the UNIX applications programs were written in C. The real beauty of C lies in the fact that it is not tied to any one machine or system. Programs written in C for one machine can generally be transferred to others or may run on these with a few modifications.

Heretofore, C has been relegated to the "big" machines, the minicomputers. Recently, however, compilers have been cropping up for many of the popular personal computers, and it is to these users that this book is addressed.

Due to the major uses of C outside of the personal microcomputer world, its historical past might be considered a bit dim by most of us. Certain user formats have developed among system-level programmers that are more of an "underground" occurrence than anything else, which has to do with the way the language is handled on a line-by-line basis and relates to the number of white spaces, or indentations, assigned to any particular program line. Actually, none of these conventions are mandatory for the proper operation of a program written in C. This language is very forgiving of many different formatting methods. These so-called conventions have been developed by the system-level programmers themselves and passed among this small group. For this reason, you will see C language programs presented in several different forms, depending on who is writing them. Again, I am speaking here only of the white spaces and indentations present on each line. To relate this to BASIC, we might say that one programmer types in a line number and then adds two spaces before entering a statement, three spaces before entering a function, and four spaces before entering a nonexecutable line, such as REM. From the standpoint of a program run, the white spaces mean nothing, but in C certain white-space configurations have simply come about. Most programmers accustomed to working with C feel a bit uncomfortable when these formatting rules are ignored or changed.

From a tutorial standpoint, however, most of us who learn new languages and have been initially trained in BASIC find the hodgepodge of white spaces to be a bit confusing. Do those white spaces have to be there?

Does this bracket have to be placed one space in from the other bracket? The answer to these questions, in most instances, is no. C language does not contain a large number of formal restrictions, which would certainly be the case if the white spaces were a main concern. The lack of these formalities or restrictions makes it an extremely versatile language for all levels of programmers. As is the case with any limited structure environment, however, certain conventions have been established by those who frequent it.

The introductory chapters in this book, which discuss C language programs, have simply ignored most of these conventions. As a matter of fact, the programs presented in many instances will more closely resemble the formatting of BASIC programs, only without the line numbers. As the discussion goes further, the format will more closely resemble conventional C programming uses.

When one begins to research the past of C language, it almost seems mystical. Indeed, the language seems to have sprung from nowhere, and after its inception, to have been used by some secret cult or society. This may be due in part to the intensity of the persons who were very involved in using this language. These were the system-level programmers with masters and doctorates or with the life experience equivalent of these degrees. Many such persons often have difficulty relaying their vast stores of knowledge and experience in a way that those of us who have no inkling whatsoever of all that is involved can understand.

In researching this book, I was very fortunate to be assisted by Richard Balocca of SuperSoft, Inc. He has been programming in C for half a decade and was able to provide some insight into how this language came about. He attributes the development of C language and the UNIX operating system to the competitiveness of a small group of programmers at Bell Laboratories in Murray Hill, New Jersey. This competitiveness would seem to be restricted to the individuals themselves, competing one against the other on a mostly friendly basis. Apparently, when they were building UNIX, one would take up where the other left off, then another and another, until the cycle was complete, and the first one would start in again. This development has been described as a fermentation of diversified ideas. There was no lack of criticism among the developers regarding improvements. Naturally, the names Brian W. Kernighan and Dennis M. Ritchie come into the picture as members of this group, but another name stands out quite prominently: Ken Thompson, who was heavily involved in developing a Pascal program at the University of California at Berkeley. He is described by many programmers as the best in the world, and no one will deny he is great. After leaving Berkeley, Thompson became involved in the MULTICS project, which was a joint venture of Massachusetts Institute of Technology, the Honeywell Corporation, and Bell Laboratories. Bell later dropped out of the project, but MULTICS was eventually developed for the

GE-645 computer and also for the Honeywell 6045. MULTICS provides its many users with a powerful means of managing and sharing files. The name MULTICS may have figured very prominently in naming the UNIX operating system. Ken Thompson's work with MULTICS before Bell dropped out had reached a point where he had written an editor called QED, which is still probably used to this day on MULTICS.

However, once Bell Labs and MULTICS were no longer associated, Ken Thompson sought other avenues to fill the void. He was able to latch onto a DEC PDP-7, and in his spare time, he put together an operating system. It was written in assembler, and it was called UNIX. It is seriously presumed by many system-level programmers that the name UNIX actually stands for castrated MULTICS. This may or may not be a fact, but UNIX was certainly designed along the lines of a single-user MULTICS. The first UNIX was a single-user version.

While it would appear that Thompson may have entered this project on a personal basis—and most likely alone—at some point in the development, he began to attract attention and quite a bit of interest. Somewhere during the development, Dennis Ritchie came in on this project. During this same time, the UNIX operating system was transferred from the surplus PDP-7 to a surplus PDP-11. (In this context, *surplus* simply means the machines were not actively being used by Bell Laboratories.)

As this sequence of events was occurring, Ken Thompson wrote an interpreter for a language called B, which is a language very similar to BCPL, the latter being a portable language that made some fairly simple assumptions about the machine on which it was operating. As a result, programs could be ported from machine to machine fairly easily. A comparison between BCPL and C language today would show quite a few similarities. Thompson enjoyed the fact that code could be written in a fairly nice manner and easily with BCPL, and therefore refined a portion of it, which gave B. The reason B was chosen as the name for this language is probably due to the fact that it was a very small and simple part of BCPL; therefore, the first letter of the mother language was chosen as its name.

When Dennis Ritchie entered the picture, he became interested in the interpreter which Ken Thompson had written, and he ended up writing a compiler that he called C. The name was not chosen because C follows B in the alphabet, but because it is the second letter in BCPL, and the compiler he had written was a logical progression from this mother language. If we were to trace the roots of C, we might find this:

$$PL1 \rightarrow BCPL \rightarrow B \rightarrow C$$

Further refinements of C language might result in another language called P, rather than D. The next would be L.

Getting back on track, UNIX was now written in assembler language and had been transferred to the PDP-11. One almost gets the impression that there was a race among this small group at Murray Hill to do something new and different with a system that had apparently sprung out of one man's fantasies. The next logical step was to rewrite UNIX in C. This was done and it apparently did not take so very long to make the conversion. Of course, UNIX was in single-user form, and even this was addressed. A multi-user UNIX was developed using a simple recoding. When this new system was brought up, it ran rather quickly.

To further illustrate this competition to which we alluded earlier, it is rumored that about this time, there was a very strong competition between those at Murray Hill who were BLISS-oriented and the Dennis Ritchie people, who were C-oriented. BLISS is a complex language that consists of a tremendously large number of operators. The competition involved the writing of an optimal code for the PDP-11. As it turns out, BLISS probably won, but due to this competition, the C optimizer is classified as excellent by many programmers. Basically, C language grew because it was a fairly optimal way to use the PDP-11 and because it has an amazing simplicity coupled with a high degree of expressiveness.

From a system-level programmer's standpoint, C is desirable because a few lines of this code corresponded to an approximate number of lines of assembler. In other words, one could judge overall program size by comparing codes, avoiding the possibility of one line of C code suddenly blossoming into thousands of lines of assembler. C language allows the programmer to retain a ''feel'' of how much code is being generated.

At the time when C was first introduced, it was extremely rare to see anything as complex as an operating system written in a high-level language. This, of course, was the case with the final versions of UNIX, which were written almost entirely in C. You will recall the earlier versions were first written in assembler. Certainly, some operating systems had been partially written (to a small degree) in high-level language, but the major portions and particularly the device drivers were written in assembler. Again, UNIX uses C almost entirely, and even the device drivers are written in this high-level language. At the time, this was highly unusual. The reason for the extensive use of C in UNIX is the efficiency of this language, and the fact that it allowed the programmer constantly to rate how well a particular programming problem was being tackled in terms of machine cycles.

Of course, all this discussion involves C language and the systems programmer. What about the average microcomputer user? Well, we cannot really say average because this individual is relegated entirely to a BASIC interpreter. How about those slightly above-average microcomputer programmers who may have expanded outward to a BASIC compiler, FORTRAN, Pascal, or even a COBOL compiler? How does C language fit in to this auspicious group who use personal computers? Again, I am speaking here of the person who is not employed as a computer programmer, but who may use a personal computer in some business applications and at home. The answer: There is already a small underground movement of people who are writing many of their programs in C. Back on the systems level again, many of the commercial software producers are rewriting nearly 100 percent of their current offerings in C. The same percentile applies to all new offerings. Some professional systems level programmers do admit to seeing limited usage of C among microcomputer hobbyists. There are some problems, however. Most C compilers do not perform functions such as array bounds checking. This could be implemented, but in most cases, it is not. Of course, the main problem lies in the fact that there is no good interpreter available at present for this language. While the interpreter slows execution time, it does speed the time required actually to write and then begin executing the program. There is a faction at SuperSoft, Inc. who would like to see that company produce a C interpreter for various machines. It is certainly not a top priority project at this time. This would not be a terribly difficult project, so the software could be sold for a reasonable price. However, while the language is becoming more and more popular among system-level programmers, it is still a bit of a mystery to the average personal computer user. The demand is not there at the present time. But anything could happen in the near future.

Will C become the standard programming language of today's systems specialists? The answers are many and varied. Some feel the answer is yes, while others say no. One individual with whom I spoke surmised that it would, but that it too would certainly be improved upon in the very near future. When persons ask what language they should learn to be most effective as a systems programmer, there is no real answer. C may come closer than all of the others, for a very strange reason. While the language does have its faults, it generally does not teach bad programming habits, which some of the other high-level languages do out of necessity of operation. Pascal is a good example of this. Of course, many professional programmers come down hard on BASIC because it too teaches some bad programming habits, but only in relation to assembler or machine language methods. The fact of the matter is that most people who use BASIC will not need to go further as far as languages are concerned. One must realize that these criticisms are usually leveled by persons who have what could only be classified as an intimate understanding of computer workings. Most of these people are capable of programming in the language of the machine itself; the rest of us are limited to some human-oriented languages that make the going much easier, but also limit operations at the same time. Perhaps C is the happy medium between machine language and the true high-level language.

The fact of the matter is that while BASIC provides reasonably good understanding of what is taking place regarding a typical human impression of a computer run, it really gives us no idea of what is taking place on a machine language level. For this reason, many high-level programmers become utterly confused after writing a few short lines in BASIC because they are more accustomed to thinking of machine operations on a machine level rather than concentrating mainly on the commands that bring about an ultimate result.

It is to be hoped that this discussion has given you a bit of insight into how C came about. If even half of the bits and pieces of information that have filtered back to me, along with the multitude of rumors, are true, it would appear that C was not developed as the result of a major corporation's attempt to produce a highly salable commodity for a booming business and scientific market. Rather, it all started with a handful of highly professional programmers who, at first, "toyed" with the idea of a simple language that suited their needs and yet would provide the fewest restrictions and the ulimate in machine compatibility. Nor did C grow from only one person. It grew from the minds and imaginations of a handful who were in friendly competition with each other. They practiced the fine art of one-upmanship and the entire industry benefitted. Unlike almost every other language popular today, C did not grow out of an industry need; rather, it blossomed from personal desire, a desire to come up with something that was better. One might say that C sprang from a collection of benign ego trips that pitted a handful of individuals against the rest of the computer world in an effort which saw the former trying to develop something that was better rather than bigger. While some may argue, many will aver that this small group was victorious.

2 THE SUPERSOFT C COMPILER

When I was assigned to write a book to introduce microcomputer users to C programming language, my first task was to locate a compiler that would allow present owners of microcomputers to run programs in C on their machine. In explaining this compiler, however, it is necessary to backtrack a bit and explain exactly what a compiler is and why it is necessary. Most persons who have had experience with personal computers started programming in BASIC using a BASIC interpreter built into the ROM of the machine. An interpreter and a compiler are quite a bit different. Both are programmed, but the interpreter translates the instructions of the source program on a one-by-one basis and executes them immediately. The interpreter operates directly on the source program in memory.

Now, it must be understood that your computer—and for that matter, any computer—does not understand any language you program into it, other than machine language. This is the final language, which is in binary form. All other languages, such as BASIC, FORTRAN, COBOL, and C must ultimately be compiled or translated into binary code before entering the processor. Machine language is binary language, and all programs, whether used with interpreters or compilers, end up in machine language before they can be used by the computer.

Machine language, unlike other languages, is not oriented toward the average human being who does not have a doctorate in computer science. In BASIC, C, and many other languages, when we want to display information on the screen, we use a statement or function, such as PRINT (BASIC) or printf (C). These words themselves give an indication of what is to occur. However, when they reach the processor, these words become a series of binary numbers, which tell the processor to do a myriad of jobs. If we could all program in machine language, there would be no need for any other language.

However, this is neither reasonable nor practical. Therefore, languages have been developed that allow for a more conventional and easy interface of humans and computers. Some languages specifically address scientific and technical applications. This does not mean that other types of applications are not possible with the language, only that it is specially tailored to meet the needs of persons working in a specific field. Many others are very general languages. BASIC is a good example of a general language, in that its uses are extremely varied. Of course, this means a compromise in certain areas.

Again, most personal computers come equipped with a BASIC interpreter. Each time a program is written in BASIC and run, the interpreter reads it line by line, converts each line to machine language, and runs each line before moving on to the next. This last statement is not completely accurate but it does give the general idea. When an interpreter is used, conversion of BASIC program lines to machine language must take place constantly, each time the program is used. Due to this constant conversion routine, BASIC interpreters are rather slow when compared with machine language programs and/or compilers.

A compiler is quite different from an interpreter, although it too must convert a language into machine language. However, the compiler does not do this each time the program is run. As a matter of fact, the compiler is not even a part of the program run, as is the interpreter. A program is written in a high-level language and is then compiled. This takes place before the program can be run at all. The compiled program may be straight machine language; more often, it is assembly language. It is difficult to explain in easy terms the differences between machine language and assembly language. For the sake of this discussion, let's consider the two to be almost identical.

At this point, you probably don't see a great deal of difference between an interpreter and a compiler, since they both accept one language and convert it to another which the machine understands. The big difference lies in the fact that the interpreter makes its conversions on a line-by-line basis *as* the program is being run, whereas the compiler converts the entire program into a form the machine can understand on a one-time basis *before* the program is run. Once the program has been compiled, the compiler need never go through this process again. When the program is run, there is no further conversion (at least in the framework of this discussion). Therefore, the program is executed much faster, since there are no conversion steps to tie up the machine's processing time.

When you are writing programs in BASIC, you must first turn your machine on and allow ROM to get you into a BASIC programming mode (or read it from diskette). You are then free to begin writing your programs. One of the first questions I'm usually asked by someone who's using a compiler for the first time is, "How do I input the program information?"

You do this using the line editor. The exact method of calling this program will depend on your machine. For running programs included in this book, I used an IBM Personal Computer with 128K memory and the MS-DOS operating system. Here, the line editor is called EDLIN and is entered by simply typing EDLIN followed by the name of the program you wish to create. Again, the line editor can actually be used to edit and/or create a program. A line editor or editor can usually create new source files and save them, delete, edit, insert, and display program lines, and update old files.

Using the IBM Personal Computer, you simply type EDLIN followed by the name of the program. When the EDLIN mode is entered, typing the letter *I* will put you in the mode used to write new programs. A line number will appear (starting at 1), and you begin inputting your program just as you would in BASIC. The line number is there to help you keep track of your input. The numbers will not be displayed in a program that is committed to diskette file. Other machines may format their editors in a different manner, but this general procedure will apply to most.

If you have a machine and an editor, you can be writing C programs right now without ever having to resort to a compiler. Don't be too over-joyed, because without the compiler, you will have no opportunity what-soever to actually run the programs you write. Using your microcomputer and most editors, you can write programs in any language you desire, but you're going to need compilers to allow them to be run on that machine.

Again, an interpreter converts each program line from one language to machine language. This conversion process must take place each and every time the program is run. Therefore, a BASIC program written under a BASIC interpreter is never in an understandable form in regard to the microprocessor, as far as a line-by-line program listing is concerned. When a compiler is used, it converts a program written in a high-level language to one that is understandable by the microprocessor. The conversion takes place once and only once; from then on, the program you wrote in that language is now contained in binary form. No further conversions are necessary.

The SuperSoft C Compiler

C programming language is new. However, its popularity is growing by leaps and bounds. This is especially true for software companies, many of which are now rewriting much of the software they sell in C. This does not mean that you will have to have a C compiler to run all of the popular programs of the future. This simply means that the software programmers are writing in C. The programs are then compiled (at the company), and when you receive them on diskette, they are ready to run on your machine.

Due to the newness of C and its traditional applications in the UNIX operating system—and, more specifically, with large business computers—it was a bit difficult at first to locate a company that offered a C compiler. My assignment was even more difficult because every reader does not own the same type of microcomputer. Thus, I had to locate a company which offered a C compiler for the most popular microcomputers of today.

Fortunately, I received some information from SuperSoft, Inc., in Champaign, Illinois. I was delighted to find that this company offers a C compiler designed for many different microprocessors, and, thus, for microcomputers. Machines equipped with the 8080, 8085, Z80, 8086, 8088, or Z8000 CPU's can generally be used with this compiler. Their compilers operate under CP/M, except for Z8000 systems, which use ZMOS. Their compilers for machines using the 8086/8088 microprocessor can be ordered to operate under CP/M-86 or MS-DOS. As of this writing, the SuperSoft C compiler would seem to be the most versatile offered in regard to machine compatibility. A phone call to SuperSoft was quite productive, in that I was able to obtain the software package for my machine, along with the technical support of the SuperSoft staff. I should say from the onset that this company has provided a wealth of information. Also, it should be understood that their C compiler is in the process of being upgraded, so many of the functions that are not fully implemented in the package available as of this writing will be included in the 1.2 version.

The SuperSoft package accepts most of the C language with a few exceptions. The company is committed to implementing the full C language as this becomes possible, and their customers will receive notices as updates are available. The 1.1 version of the SuperSoft C compiler, which was used as the model for this book, does not support TYPEDEF declarations, LONG, FLOAT, and DOUBLE data types, declaration and use of bit fields, and initialization. Other differences will be noted in later chapters.

The following is a description of the SuperSoft C compiler, which has been reprinted from the SuperSoft C Compiler User's Manual © 1983, SuperSoft.*

The SuperSoft C compiler is a self-compiling, optimizing, two-pass compiler generating a final output file in assembly source code. It is adaptable for a variety of operating systems and central processing units. Due to the inherent portability of the C language and its particular implementation in the SuperSoft C compiler, configurations for other operating systems and machines can be relatively easily and rapidly developed.

A wealth of user-callable functions are supplied with SuperSoft C. These include many UNIX compatible functions, allowing the porting of source between UNIX C and SuperSoft C with few, if any, source changes. A full, standard I/O package (stdio) is provided. This package allows file I/O that is independent of the natural record size of the target system. For instance, under CP/M, a SuperSoft C program may open a file, seek to any byte in the program, and then close the file. The appropriate byte and only the appropriate byte will be changed by this sequence of operations. Beyond that, porting services are available from SuperSoft.

Writing the SuperSoft C compiler in the language it implements not only has facilitated its development, but also has provided the most direct means of testing it. It has undergone many other extensive tests, including those resulting from its use in most of SuperSoft's programming projects. As a result, SuperSoft C has been tested on tens of thousands of unique lines of C source code.

As a result of the optimizations performed, the code generated by the

*Courtesy of SuperSoft, Inc.

compiler has spatial and temporal efficiency adequate for system-level, as well as application-level, programming. One measure of its efficiency is that for at least one operating system, CP/M, the entire I/O interface of the compiler is written in SuperSoft C, with the exception of a ten-line procedure in assembly code required as a link to the operating system.

Design decisions made with regard to code generation allow the Super-Soft C compiler to generate rather good code for subroutine entry and exit. These decisions allow for true register variables, even on machines with few registers. (Specifically, on the 8080 series, SuperSoft C uses the BC register pair as a true register variable).

The SuperSoft C compiler is a modular two-pass compiler. (On some machines, the optimization and code generation are split into individual phases. In this case, the compiler is a three-pass compiler.) Each pass is performed by a separate and distinct section of the compiler. This confers certain important advantages. Dividing the compiler into two self-contained programs allows it to run with a relatively small amount of available memory and still support most of the C language. This modular structure also leads to a clean interface between the first pass, or Parser (CC), and the optional optimization pass (COD2COD) and the final pass, or Code Generator (C2). The output file of the first pass simply becomes the input file of the second. Modularity also facilitates adapting the compiler to other machines and operating systems because the first module is machine- and system-independent and only portions of the second need be changed.

The compiler's first pass (CC) accepts as input a SuperSoft C source code file and parses it. As output, it generates a file in an intermediate code known as Universal code, or U-code (implying code not specific to any one system or machine). One of the design specifications of the compiler is that the output of both of its passes must be intelligible to a human being, so U-code may be viewed and modified using an ordinary text editor.

A machine-independent, U-code–to–U-code optimizer (COD2COD) is supplied with the compiler. In the case of the 8080 series compilers, this pass is combined with the code-generation pass (C2). This pass accepts as input the U-code file generated by (CC). The input file undergoes a complex optimization process involving global code rearrangement within functions, as well as reiterative local code transformations within a "peephole," or window, of a certain number of lines of code. The code-generation process (C2) produces a final output file in assembly language.

Several benefits result from the choice of assembly code as the final output of the compiler, some of particular value to the system-level programmer. Because the code generated is intentionally not specific to any one of the assemblers in use on a given machine, practically any hardware-compatible assembler (including absolute as well as relocating assemblers) may be used. Thus, the output of this compiler can be integrated into any software system already written in, or compatible with, assembly source code. The programmer can also insert lines of assembly code directly into a C source file by bracketing them with the compiler directives # ASM and # ENDASM. Lines so inserted are not optimized or altered in any way by the compiler.

Use of assembly source code also satisfies SuperSoft's design specification requiring that the output of both passes be intelligible to a human being. The resulting readability of the compiler's output facilitates debugging and allows any user to see the kind of code generated by the compiler. Thus, the programmer need not take for granted that the code generated is what was desired and may either alter the source code or "hand polish" the generated code to make the result more suitable for a particularly demanding application.

A major trade-off in the design of any compiler is in the time required to compile a program versus the time required to execute it. Since one of SuperSoft's primary goals was to generate code efficient enough for system-level programming, they have emphasized speed of execution at the expense of speed of compilation. (Certain optimizations performed by C2 require time proportional to the square of the size—the number of U-code instructions—of the largest C function to be optimized.) Optimization can be turned off for faster compilation. This emphasis, while increasing the turn-around time during program development, does make the compiler useful for a far broader range of programming tasks. The SuperSoft C compiler is unique, in that it allows you to do efficient system-level programming with structure and clarity on a relatively small hardware system.

SuperSoft provides a lengthy user's manual with its C compiler. However, if you have never used a compiler before, you may run into a few problems in understanding the information, although the early part of this chapter will clear up most of them. The files included on your C compiler diskettes will vary depending on which machine you own. In any event, the first three programs on the A diskette are the ones used to convert your C program into assembly language.

Again, the SuperSoft C package is a two-pass compiler. The first pass produces an intermediate code, while the second pass contains both the translater and the optimizer. The IBM version that I use is technically a three-pass compiler, in that the first pass establishes a file name COD, the second produces the actual intermediate code, and the third provides the assembly language output. Technically, this version would probably still be classified as a two-pass compiler, although the first pass is handled in two separate machine actions. The intermediate code is optimized and assembly code is output to disk file. The optimizer typically results in a 40% code reduction. This means that compiled object code will run nearly as fast as that written in assembler. Compile-time options include listing files, console output, syntax checking, and others. This particular package requires a minimum of 48K memory, but more is recommended. Incidentally, Super-Soft offers their C compiler package for all microprocessors except the 8086 for $275. Those with the Intel 8086 chips, which include the 8088 found in the IBM Personal Computer, must order the 8086 version, which cost $500 (prices in effect as of January, 1983).

With the compiler comes the complete source code to most of the run-time system. There are 85 standard library functions, which are outlined in a later chapter. Figure 2–1 provides a listing of these functions.

Again, the 8086 version of SuperSoft C was used as a model for this book. This chapter overviews some of the operating techniques using this particular compiler. If you have a different machine or are using a different software package, this overview may not apply directly to your operations, but all operations using the SuperSoft C compiler should be quite similar.

Once your program has been written in C, there are three programs on the compiler diskette used to make the conversion to assembly language. For the MS-DOS compiler, these are CC.EXE, COD2COD.EXE, and C2I86.EXE. Other machines will probably use only CC and C2 to accomplish the same thing. Let's assume that the name of the C program that has been written using EDLIN and the IBM Personal Computer with MS-DOS is called PGM.C. Here is how this program will be compiled. Type:

```
CC PGM.C
COD2COD PGM.COD
C2I86 PGM.U + LINK + MSDOS
```

Each one of these actions will cause the diskette drive to be activated. If your program is short, it will take only a few seconds for the rewrite process to be completed and the DOS prompt to appear on the screen. The first conversion (CC) reads your program and converts it to a diskette file called PGM.COD. The COD2COD file converts the PGM.COD file to PGM.U. Finally, the C2I86 file (the second pass of the compiler) converts the PGM.U file to PGM.ASM. The compilation process is now complete.

However, it is not ready to run yet on the IBM Personal Computer, although the job of the Supersoft compiler package is over for the moment. In order to run the assembly language program on the IBM PC using MS-DOS, you must also have the IBM Macro-Assembler software package available from IBM for about $100. The C compiler has converted your C language program to its assembly language equivalent, but now you must assemble this package in a way that will create an object file. To do this, you simply input MASM PGM.ASM. MASM is a file on the macro-assembler diskette that will assemble your assembly language program. You're not

alloc	free	isupper	seek
atoi	fscanf	iswhite	setexit
bdos	getc	kbhit	setmem
bios	getchar	movmem	sleep
brk	gets	open	sprintf
ccall	getval	outp	srand
ccalla	getw	pause	sscanf
close	index	peek	strcat
cpmver	initb	poke	strcmp
creat	initw	printf	strcpy
evnbrk	inp	putc	streq
exec	isalnum	putchar	strlen
execl	isalpha	puts	strncat
exit	isascii	putw	strncpy
fabort	iscntrl	qsort	tell
fclose	isdigit	rand	tolower
fflush	islower	read	topofmem
fgets	isnumeric	reset	toupper
fopen	isprint	rindex	ungetc
fprintf	ispunct	sbrk	ungetchar
fputs	isspace	scanf	unlink
			write

Figure 2-1 Functions Supported in The C Compiler Package from SuperSoft.

through yet. The output from the MASM operation will be PGM.OBJ. You're now getting very close. This object file must be converted to an executable file (EXE) by using the LINKER program found in IBM DOS. It seems like a very complicated process, and to those who have never used a compiler, a macro-assembler, and a linker, it takes a bit of getting used to.

Linking the LINK program contained on your IBM diskette combines separately produced object modules into a program that is directly executable. To explain this further, however, it is necessary to return to the C compiler. The next chapter will tell you how to actually write programs in C language, but it is necessary that you know ahead of time how to run these programs so that they may be tested as soon as they are complete. This is the purpose of this chapter. Each time you write a new C program, you will have to go through all of the steps of compilation already discussed.

The LINK program links object modules. This means it acts upon any file that is named and has a designation of .OBJ. In C language, there are separate files making up what is known as the *library*. The library contains the definitions for functions that are used in any program. The classification of functions will be dealt with later, but to be brief, there are five library files, which are named STDIO, ALLOC, FUNC, CRUNT2, and FORMATIO. You will find these on your C compiler diskettes in two different forms. One set contains OBJ extensions, while others contain C extensions. The ones with C extensions may be called by your C language program and are compiled along with it. The others with OBJ extensions have already been compiled and may be *linked* with your compiled and assembled C language programs. The use manual supplied with the SuperSoft C compiler goes into this in great detail.

To avoid as much confusion as possible, the following method should be used to link your C program object module with the library functions that will be needed. Type:

LINK PREF + ALLOC + FUNC + STDIO + CRUNT2 + FORMATIO +
PGM + POST,PGM;

Two other files, PREF and POST, normally precede and follow the library files and your C program. At the time of this writing, SuperSoft was making some changes and in some versions, PREF may not be used. Consult your manual for further details.

This is not the most efficient way of getting an object program into executable form, because all the files linked to PGM probably would not be needed. The library files simply define the function in a manner that the machine can understand. If you write a program that does not contain any function defined in a certain file, it is not necessary to link this file with the other object modules. The method shown here, however, assures that any correctly written program can be successfully linked. Using this method, only the library files with OBJ extensions are used. The others with C extensions are meant to be compiled with the program you write. This makes for far more efficient use of memory storage space, but the purpose of this book is to introduce you to C programming language. This involves writing a number of short programs, which are then compiled and run on your machine. If you compile the library files at the same time your short program is being compiled, the process takes far longer. In some instances, it can take 10 minutes or so to perform the entire process. By using the already-compiled program provided on diskette by SuperSoft, the amount of time needed to compile and assemble the program and finally, to link it, is greatly reduced.

Again, I am speaking here of a specific compiler package from one company. Other packages may not include the previously compiled library files, but it will probably be to your best advantage to compile and assemble each of them and then use the LINK program as shown. This method seems to work best because of the efficiency involved in compilation speeds. The beginning C programmer can quickly see the results of his or her program while the line-by-line input information is still fresh.

To recap, here are the steps in running programs written in C programming language:

1. Write your program using the line editor (EDLIN in MS-DOS).
2. Begin the compilation process by typing CC and then the name of your program.
3. Type COD2COD and then the name of your program followed by a .COD extension.

4. Type C2I86 + LINK + MSDOS and then the name of your program, followed by a .U extension.
5. Using the Macro-Assembler program, type MASM and the name of your program twice, separated by commas. (i.e., MASM PGM,PGM;)
6. Using the LINK program, type LINK PREF + ALLOC + FUNC + STDIO + CRUNT2 + FORMATIO + (name of program) + POST, (name of program);

The output from the LINK program should be PGM.EXE, assuming that the name of the original compiled program was PGM. The total compilation method and assembly portion seems to be a bit more complex for 8086 CPU systems than for other types of microprocessors. In any event, consult the software documentation provided by the company who supplies your compiler to answer any questions, especially about methods that may differ from those outlined here for my machine.

Fortunately, SuperSoft supplies a batch file with their package, which can greatly simplify the entire process. As a matter of fact, if you have an IBM Personal Computer (and, most probably, any other system) equipped with dual disk drives, only a single command need be issued to handle the entire compilation, assembly, and linking process. Figure 2-2 shows a printout of the batch file contained on my diskette. I did make some alterations to the second line from the bottom in order to link the precompiled object modules that make up the library files to the object module containing the C program. You can write your own batch file for the IBM PC along similar lines. This batch file assumes that all programs you write in C language will contain the extension of .C.

Looking at the batch file on a line-by-line basis, this is what happens. First, you type in the name of your program (while in DOS) without the extension. Let's assume that the program to be compiled is stored on diskette as SAMP1.C. To start the process, you type C SAMP1. The letter C is simply the name of the batch file selected by SuperSoft. If it were named BATCHER.BAT, you would type BATCHER SAMP1. On the SuperSoft file, the batch program is named C.BAT. As soon as you input C SAMP1, everything else is automatic. The first line in this program is CC %1.C. In DOS,

```
CC %1.C
COD2COD %1.COD
ERASE %1.COD
C2I86 +LINK +MSDOS %1.U
ERASE %1.U
MASM %1,%1;
ERASE %1.ASM
A:LINK B:ALLOC+FUNC+FORMATIO+CRUNT2+STDIO+%1+POST,%1;
ERASE %1.OBJ
```

Figure 2-2   The Author's Batch File for Compilation.

this means to load file CC.EXE. The %1 calls up the name that you typed in immediately following the letter C when you called the batch program. The .C extension is tacked on to the end of the program name. Put more simply, when the first program line is executed in DOS, it is the exact equivalent of typing in CC SAMP1.C. You will recognize this as the first step in compilation of a C program using the method previously outlined. In every case, %1 indicates that the program name is to be substituted.

The second line in the batch program starts the second step in compilation. It is the equivalent of inputting COD2COD SAMP1.COD. You can now see why you type in only the name of the program following the batch file name without the extension. During the compilation process, the extension changes from .C to .COD to .U to .ASM to .OBJ, and finally, to .EXE. In each case, the batch program changes the extension for you automatically.

The third line in this program is quite important for making the most efficient use of diskette storage space. Following the CC portion of compilation, another file, called SAMP1.COD, is added to the diskette. During the next step of compilation, the information in SAMP1.COD is put through a process that produces another file, named SAMP1.U, on diskette. At this juncture, the old SAMP1.COD file is no longer needed for anything. It simply takes up disk space. The third line in the batch program, however, erases the SAMP1.COD file, thus clearing disk space for any other files that may be written during the compilation process.

The fourth line calls the C2I86 program, and the old SAMP1.U file is immediately erased. The sixth line in the batch program invokes the macroassembler and again follows the previously discussed manual compilation process. Following this, the SAMP1.ASM file is removed from diskette, as an object file (.OBJ) has been formed from its data.

The next line is the one that I altered in the original C.BAT file supplied with my compiler package. This line is used to link all the object modules together to produce an executable file. (This will be discussed later in more detail.) The final line erases the SAMP1.OBJ file, which is no longer needed. The result of this entire batch-processing maneuver is the creation of five new files from the original SAMP1.C file. However, each file is erased when it is no longer needed. The end result will be two files. One is the original SAMP1.C, and the other is the executable file, SAMP1.EXE. To run the program, you now type SAMP1, and execution will begin. Any file in DOS with an EXE extension is automatically loaded and executed in DOS when its name is typed following the DOS prompt.

Now, let's discuss the second line from the bottom of this program. You must remember that I tailored this program specially to satisfy my methods of compilation. My computer is equipped with two 320K disk drives. I wanted to reduce the work load (especially the switching of disk-

ettes) as much as possible. The IBM Macro-Assembler will automatically
return to DOS when its run is complete. This means that the DOS diskette
must be available in one of the disk drives or a message will appear at the end
of the assembler run telling you to insert a proper DOS diskette in one of the
drives and press any key. Some of the programs I was compiling required
large amounts of time, and it was quite bothersome to have to sit in front of
the machine watching the drives spin and waiting for a prompt to tell me that
it was time to insert another diskette.

   Here's how the entire situation was solved using the IBM Personal
Computer. All of the EXE, OBJ, and ASM files on the SuperSoft C compiler diskettes were copied to a single 320K (double-sided) diskette. The
MASM program from the Macro-Assembler diskette was copied to the 320K
diskette as well. There was enough space left to include the link file from the
DOS diskette as well, but this did not allow the room needed to perform
compilations, which involves writing additional files to the same diskette.
Therefore, the link program is simply pulled from the DOS diskette, which
must be in one of the drives anyway. Again, the diskette I made up by copy-
ing files from all the others contains the major C compiler files, library files,
and all other files needed for the compilation process (EXE, OBJ, and ASM
files). This diskette also contains the MASM file from the IBM Macro-
Assembler package. This diskette was placed in the second drive (drive B).
The DOS diskette resides in drive A.

   When I want to write a program in C language, I first bring up DOS
(drive A) and then type EDLIN B:SAMP1.C (assuming the name of the program is SAMP1). This allows me to call up the EDLIN program in drive A in
order to write a program called SAMP1.C, which will be written to drive B.
The end result is a new file on the B diskette named SAMP1.C. Once the file
has been written, I then switch I/O to drive B (type B: and press Enter) and
then invoke the batch processing file (C.BAT).

   Now let's get back to the link portion of the batch file. Remember, the
link file is on a diskette in drive A, while the object files are found on drive B.
As shown in Figure 2–2, the link portion of this program reads:

A:LINK B:ALLOC + FUNC + FORMATIO + CRUNT2 + STDIO +
%1 + POST,%1;

This line tells the computer to switch I/O to drive A, access the link program,
and apply it to the files in drive B, as outlined. This makes use of the files on
both diskettes without the need for manual switching. You will notice that
my link line does not contain a PREF file, because I was using a package being developed by SuperSoft that did not require the PREF file, as all the
others did. The package you are supplied might require PREF, and then
again, it might not. Consult your owner's manual if in doubt.

The batch file lines discussed here are exactly like those contained in my original program, except for the link line, which was modified to suit my individual operating needs. By inserting the DOS diskette in drive A and the compiler diskette in drive B, the system seems to work best. The compilation process begins with I/O switched to drive B where the C.BAT file is called. The B diskette is used to access all files up to and including MASM. When the assembly of the source code has been completed, however, DOS will be called again, but the DOS diskette in drive A will automatically be accessed and will send control back to drive B for the erasure of the ASM file. The next program line then sends control to drive A to call the LINK program to complete the final stages of producing an executable program.

There is one problem with this method of compilation. Any one of the compilation and assembly stages can produce an error message. Unfortunately, by the time the error message appears, the previous file has been erased. This means that you have to go back into your C program, correct the errors, and then compile all over again. This is no problem when the errors are actually in the C program, but a similar situation can develop when a certain file is not available on a diskette called by your batch program. This assumes that you are using a batch system different from the one outlined here. In any event, there is no great harm done—only the loss of a little time.

To give you an idea of what a typical compilation process looks like using the SuperSoft C compiler, the IBM Personal Computer, and the batch program discussed here, Figure 2-3 shows a complete printout of the screen messages that occur during the compilation of a program called SAMP1.C. This is the process that has been previously described, but remember, it was necessary to issue only one command—C SAMP1—to effect the entire compilation, assembly, and linking. If you need to compile a lengthy program, you can simply issue the batch command and do other things not associated with the computer until your EXE file is complete.

As I pointed out earlier, the MS-DOS version of the SuperSoft C compiler used here contains an extra step because the second pass is divided into two separate sections, a code optimizer and a code generator. When using CP/M versions of this compiler, it may be necessary to issue only a single command for the second pass; in other cases, two commands will be necessary.

This chapter has only touched on the basic aspects of the multifaceted SuperSoft C compiler package. Their instruction manual will take you through the rigors of other operations that you will find necessary as your proficiency with this language increases. For the time being, the method of compilation, assembly, and linking described here may be used directly by anyone who owns the IBM personal computer and is comparably equipped. Others may use the description here as a rough guide and supplement the information provided by SuperSoft or any other company who may be supplying a compiler that operates in a similar manner.

```
B>CC samp1.C
PCDOS Run time V1.2.13  Copyright 1982 SuperSoft
C Compiler V1.1.32      Output is samp1.COD
0 compilation errors
B>COD2COD samp1.COD
PCDOS Run time V1.2.13  Copyright 1982 SuperSoft
Optimizer V1.1.13       Output is samp1.U
0 code generation errors
B>ERASE samp1.COD

B>C2I86 +LINK +MSDOS samp1.U
PCDOS Run time V1.2.13  Copyright 1982 SuperSoft
Code Gen. V1.1.1042     Output is samp1.ASM
1 temporary labels used.
0 code generation errors
B>ERASE samp1.U

B>MASM samp1,samp1;
The IBM Personal Computer MACRO Assembler
Version 1.00 (C)Copyright IBM Corp 1981


Warning Severe
Errors  Errors
0       0

B>ERASE samp1.ASM

B>A:LINK B:ALLOC+FUNC+FORMATIO+CRUNT2+STDIO+samp1+POST,samp1;

IBM Personal Computer Linker
Version 1.10 (C)Copyright IBM Corp 1982


B>ERASE samp1.OBJ

B>
B>^C
```

Figure 2-3   A Typical Compilation Run Using the Batch Program to Compile a C
Program Entitled sampl.c.

The main problem newcomers seem to have with the use of compilers
lies in the fact that they don't understand what a compiler is supposed to do.
Once this understanding is gained, however, there is an easy transition to fast
and reliable compilation of all programs.

3 PROGRAMMING IN C

Our major goal in this book is to provide detailed instructions understandable to anyone who wishes to program in C language. Certainly system-level programmers, especially those who have had ample experience with C previously, will not find this information as useful from a learning standpoint as will those programmers with much more limited experience. This book is aimed at a wide range of individuals, especially those who have been using microcomputers and, for the most part, BASIC language.

In making the switch from BASIC to any other language—including C—it is best from a teaching standpoint to make as many comparisons as possible between the known language and the one being learned. Many books that provide instruction in computer languages make comparisons to FORTRAN, PASCAL, and others. This may be due to the mistaken belief that computerists who are not employed in computer fields and look at programming as a hobby rather than a profession will always stay with BASIC. While not admitted in many circles, programmers who are experienced and conversant in languages other than BASIC sometimes look down their noses at those who use BASIC. This, of course, does not apply to those experienced programmers who have been around enough to know the advantages and disadvantages inherent in any computer language.

The microcomputerist probably has been using a BASIC interpreter, and there is quite an adjustment to make when using the same machine with a compiler for C, or—for that matter—any other computer language. This point has been addressed earlier.

Learning a new computer language is identical to learning to speak a language other than your own. It can also be equated with learning Morse code which, in itself, is a binary language. We must always reference certain aspects of the new language to those of the old. You normally think in your native language, while a mental "interpreter" makes the required conversion. However, as your proficiency in a new language increases, it is quite probable you will think in this new language quite a bit. This will not completely replace your native language, but such occurrences are more frequent as efficiency in the new language is attained.

Chances are, if you began your pursuit in the computer field using BASIC language as a tool, you will always compare any other language to this one. Certainly, if you made a quick switch from BASIC to another language and have used this new language for many years, then BASIC may not serve as a point of reference. However, most people who have used nothing but microcomputers will probably fall into the former category, so I decided to reference certain points of discussion regarding C language to BASIC in an attempt to achieve the highest level of understanding. In many instances, it's easier to make references to FORTRAN, and for those who know this language well, such references could further understanding with fewer words. It has been my experience, however, that those most familiar with FORTRAN are also quite familiar with BASIC. In fact, BASIC is as close to being a universal language to the average microcomputer user as machine language is to being a true universal language.

The programs discussed in this chapter are quite simple and accomplish very little from a practical standpoint. Looking at them tutorially, however, you should find that each provides a wealth of knowledge about specific aspects of C and can be directly applied to practical applications. I will discuss most programs on a line-by-line basis to allow you to grasp the individual units used to arrive at a sum. Unlike some texts, which provide program "segments," each program shown can be compiled and run in its entirety. There is nothing especially wrong with pulling out sections of programs, which can be discussed in regard to their own merit. However, beginning programmers sometimes get the idea that these sections are indeed working programs. If these segments are input to a machine and compiled, a long series of error messages will probably occur. If the programmer assumes this information was correct from the beginning, there can apparently be only three reasons for the refusal of the input program to compile and run: typing error, software (compiler) error, or typographical error in the book from which the program was garnered. Each program discussed in this chapter has been compiled using the SuperSoft C compiler and will run. You will also note that each program passes a visual output to the monitor screen. A number of texts discuss programs that do quite a bit on the machine level but do not give any indication of what is taking place. This is fine for those with a fairly good background in learning a new language, but not for those trying to make the difficult transition from one language to another for the first time. It is this latter group at which this book is aimed. However, as you become more experienced in C, I think you will find other chapters in this text serve as excellent reference sources.

A First Program

The first program that we will write and run in C programming language will print a simple phrase on the display screen. The phrase I have chosen is "hello, how are you." If we were using BASIC to accomplish this same task, the program might read:

10   PRINT "hello, how are you"

However, when using C, the program will look similar to the one shown in Figure 3-1. You will immediately notice the use of printf, which corresponds to the PRINT statement in BASIC. The equivalent term in C is a library

```
main()
{
printf("hello,how are you\n");
}
```

Figure 3-1 Simple Program That Demonstrates the printf Function.

function that passes output to the monitor screen unless some other output route is specified. For now, let's say that printf is equivalent to PRINT in BASIC.

What are the other functions and elements contained in this program? First, there is main ( ). This function tells the machine to begin execution. In many instances, program elements will be placed before main ( ), but following this function is the actual executable part of the C program.

On the next line, there is a symbol called a *brace,* which you have probably never used if all of your previous experience has involved BASIC. The brace marks the start of the statements that make up the functions. The function is the executable part of this program, which includes all information on the line which follows. Notice the closing brace at the end of the program. This marks the end of the function and the end of the program as well, in this instance. If you're getting confused at this point, just remember that all C programs will contain a main( ) and at least two braces, one open and one closed. As a matter of fact, we can take the program shown in Figure 3-1 and insert any number of other function lines between the braces and in place of the one currently shown. Remember, main( ) indicates the point at which execution is to begin, and the braces enclose the program function(s).

Now, let's look at the actual function line. Again, printf can be loosely compared to PRINT in BASIC, but there are marked differences. The function printf is used to pass information to the screen and must always be used with a phrase or string enclosed in parentheses and quotation marks. In this instance, the phrase is "hello, how are you." The addition of the parentheses is of no great concern to the BASIC user, who just remembers that a parenthesis must occur before the opening quotation mark and after those that close out a phrase. However, great concern is often expressed about the backward slash, followed by the letter *n.*

In C language, the slash-n sequence stands for *newline character.* When this is printed, it effectively returns the screen cursor to the left-hand side and advances one line. This is exactly equivalent to the carriage return on most computers and typewriters. In BASIC, the carriage-return/line-advance is a default state, which is triggered by the PRINT statement line. This is not true in C. Again, the slash-n sequence is effectively recognized by the machine, but when I say it is printed, I do not mean that \ n is displayed on the screen. Even though it is found within the quotation marks, it is not displayed on the screen and will simply return the cursor to the left side and advance a line.

A semicolon occurs at the end of the printf line. In C, this is used after every function line. An error message will occur if it is not included.

Since this program contains only one function line, the closing brace indicates the end of that function's execution and, in this case, the end of the program. When this program is compiled and run on your machine, the phrase "hello, how are you" should appear on the screen, the cursor should return to the left side of the screen one line down from the printed line, and the program should terminate. Using the SuperSoft compiler, any mistakes that you may have made in inputting this program should be discovered after the first pass of the compiler. Incidentally, if you should omit a semicolon at the end of a function line, the compiler error message will indicate a problem at the beginning of the next line (Missing Semicolon).

You may wish to experiment and leave off the slash-n sequence and see what happens. As a matter of fact, it's a good idea to play around with all these programs in order to provide yourself with the best education possible. Unfortunately, a compiler takes time, and it's not as easy to note the effect brought about by certain program changes in a short period of time, as when using BASIC. Each time a program line is changed (using the line editor), it is necessary to recompile the program. For a program of this size, it should take only a minute or so using the method described in an earlier chapter.

What if we wish to return the cursor to the left side of the screen without advancing a line? The sequence to handle this uses slash-r instead of slash-n. This is an easy one to remember because r can stand for *return* or *reverse*. Remember, however, that when the slash-r sequence is used, there is no line advance. As an exercise, replace the *n* in the program shown in Figure 3-1 with an *r* and recompile it. When the program is run, the same phrase will appear on the screen, and the flashing cursor will appear just below the *h* in *hello* when execution is complete. Note that no line advance has occurred.

Before moving on to the next program, let's recap a bit. Every program in C will contain a main( ), which marks the starting point of execution. It will also contain an opening brace and a closing brace to surround the program function line(s). Function lines are ended by using a semicolon. When printf is used to route information to the display screen, the display data must be enclosed in quotation marks and these, in turn, must be enclosed by parentheses. Sequence designators, which are indicated by a backward slash (\ ), indicate the start of the sequence. The letter *n* is used to return the cursor to the left side of the screen and advance one line, while the letter *r* is used to return the cursor to the left side without advancing one line. In each case, the sequence is always enclosed within the same quotation marks, which surround the phrase to be displayed on the screen. In these instances, the backward slash and any information that follows it will not be displayed on the screen.

This simple program may not look so simple, especially when we consider the limited amount of work we have done. In BASIC, only one line is required to accomplish the same thing, but you must remember that C is not BASIC—it has many capabilities that BASIC does not have and is far more useful in system-level programming. However, BASIC is an easy language to use, and its many shortcuts have been taken for granted by programmers who use this language. Most do not realize the price these shortcuts require. In other words, there is always a compromise; C sacrifices some shortcuts for an excellent overall adaptability to many different types of machines, while BASIC sacrifices a lot of this adaptability for programming ease. BASIC is an easier language to use in many ways, but its uses are very constricted.

Let's explore our program further by making a few modifications. The program shown in Figure 3-2 illustrates the two sequences discussed earlier; namely, slash-n and slash-r. This program is identical to the first in many ways. Note that there are the required main( ) and the opening and closing braces. However, this program contains two function lines and utilizes both the r and n sequence. In the first printf line, 20 spaces are included within the quotation marks, followed by the previous phrase. You will notice that this phrase is terminated with the return sequence using the r designator. When this line is written on the screen, the cursor will return to the left-hand position, but it will not advance a line.

As soon as this function line is executed, the next line is encountered. This is identical to the function line in the previous program and will display the phrase on the screen, return the cursor to the left-hand position, and advance a line. At this point, the closing brace effectively terminates the program run. Both printf lines are terminated by semicolons. In C, multistatement lines are allowed and are separated by semicolons. This is sometimes the case in BASIC, but more often than not, a colon is used to separate statements that occur on a single line.

This program was written to accomplish the printing of the phrase "hello, how are you" twice on one line. This could have been done in a different way by using one printf line, enclosing both phrases in parens and quotation marks. However, for demonstration purposes, this program is ideal. When run, the program will first print 20 spaces and then the phrase. The reverse sequence will then place a cursor at the left-hand side of this

```
hello,how are you    hello,how are you

B>type pgmr.c
main()
{
printf("                          hello,how are you\r");
printf("hello,how are you\n");
}
```

Figure 3-2   Program Demonstrating the n and r Escape Sequences.

same line, and the second printf function line will be executed. The phrase "hello, how are you" is printed in the 20 spaces that were originally printed from the previous line. The end result is "hello, how are you   hello, how are you." In the finished output (after program termination), the first phrase portion was printed after the second portion. While the first and second halves of this complex phrase appear to be identical, they were not, at least while the screen write process was taking place. The first phrase consists of twenty spaces followed by the words themselves. The second phrase contains only the words. It is written on top of the spaces which were printed by the first printf line. This effectively demonstrates the use of the r and n return sequences.

The second program made allowances for the overwrite that occurs when the second function line is executed. The first function line printed a series of spaces, which fully encompass the second phrase printing. The program shown in Figure 3-3 allows for the combination of phrases, or more appropriately, shows what happens when the return sequences are not be used properly. Here, the same situation as before is encountered. However, the number of spaces preceding the first phrase has been reduced to a point where the frontal space available on the printed line is not adequate to enclose the phrase in the second line. When this program is run, the screen displays "hello, how are you, how are you." In this case, the word *hello* originally printed when the first printf line was executed has been overwritten by the last few letters of the second printf line. This feature can sometimes be used for limited graphic (text mode) applications while using C, but most overwrites are the result of improper programming rather than intent.

```
hello,how are you,how are you

B>type pgmr.c
main()
{
printf("              hello,how are you\r");
printf("hello,how are you\n");
}
```

Figure 3-3   Program Combining Two Phrases on the Same Line.

To digress a bit, you must remember that the program you have written using the line editor must be compiled before it can be run on your machine. The Supersoft C package used to run programs included in this book on an IBM Personal Computer using MS-DOS is a two-pass compiler. Figure 3-4 shows the COD code output during the first pass. This is the way the computer sees the first program, in which it is simply to print "hello, how are you" on the screen. Once the COD file has been established, the COD2COD

```
iler V1.1.32
          D61   main
                 G26
                  B9
                   C1     1
                    B9
                     D27   printf
                            C65       4
                             B12
                              B99
                               B99
                                F98

 hello,how are you\010\000
                 C97
                  H91 printf
                   C97
                    B99
                     ;0 compilation errors


 samp1.u
```

Figure 3-4 COD Code Output During the First Pass of the Compiler.

command is used to produce a compilation in universal code. Finally, the
last pass of the compiler provides an output in assembler code. Figure 3-5
shows the universal code output, while Figure 3-6 shows the assembly version.

```
;Optimizer V1.1.13
;C Compiler V1.1.32
D61     main
G26
B9
C1      1
B9
D27     printf
C65     4
B12
H91     printf
F98     1
D96     hello,how are you\010\000
C97
C97
;0 compilation errors
;0 code gen errs ***

; End of program




DSEG    SEGMENT PARA PUBLIC 'DATA'
DSEG    ENDS
CSEG    SEGMENT PARA PUBLIC 'CODE'
```

Figure 3-5 Universal Code Output.

```
;Code Gen. V1.1.1042
; head86.lnk edit 11
DATA      GROUP    DSEG
CODE      GROUP    CSEG

DSEG      SEGMENT PARA PUBLIC 'DATA'
DSEG      ENDS

CSEG      SEGMENT PARA PUBLIC 'CODE'
          ASSUME  CS:CODE, DS:DATA, SS:DATA, ES:DATA
          EXTRN   ccstart:NEAR
          extrn        printf:NEAR
;Optimizer V1.1.13
;C Compiler V1.1.32
main      PROC NEAR
          PUBLIC  main
          mov BX,OFFSET c1+0
          push         BX
          MOV BX,1
          push         BX
          call         printf
          add SP,4
          ret
main      ENDP
CSEG      ENDS
          DSEG SEGMENT PARA PUBLIC 'DATA'
c1        EQU $
          db  104,101,108,108,111,44,104,111,119,32
          db  97,114,101,32,121,111,117,10,0

;0 compilation errors
;0 code gen errs ***
; End of program
;0 code gen errs ***
; trail86.lnk edit 11
DSEG      ENDS
          END

; End of program
```

Figure 3-6 Assembly Version of the Original Program.

Printing Numbers

In C, printf is also used to display numbers on the screen. The numbers may simply be included inside the quotation marks. In such a case, the numbers simply replace the letters. However, printf is most often used to display the numeric values of variables.

Using BASIC, one might display the value of a variable using the following program:

                    10   LET X = 14
                    20   PRINT X

In C, we do the same thing, but in a slightly different manner. Figure 3-7 shows the program that will print the value of x on the screen using printf.

```
main()
{
int x;
x=23456;
printf("%d\n",x);
}
```

Figure 3-7 The Value of *x* is Displayed on the Screen Using This Program.

First, you see the required main(), followed by the opening brace. In this example, *x* is our variable. In C, it is mandatory that the variable be defined before it is encountered within the function line or argument. Here, the variable *x* is defined as an integer using:

int x;

The next line assigns a value of 23456 to variable *x*. Again, a semicolon terminates this line.

The function line again uses printf, but notice that there are some new developments. Immediately inside the quotation mark, a percent sign (%) is followed by a *d*. This combination can best be called a *conversion specification*. The percent sign indicates where an argument is to be substituted. The argument is specified within the parentheses, but outside the quotation marks; it is separate from the latter by a comma. In this case, the value of *x* is to be substituted for the percent sign. The letter *d* indicates that the argument is to be a decimal integer. You may also see the letters *o, x, c,* and *s* substituted for the letter *d*. Whereas *d* stands for decimal, *o* indicates octal, *x* indicates hexadecimal, *c* stands for character, and *s* stands for character string. You may also see the letter *f* used as a conversion designator, although this is not currently supported in the SuperSoft C package used for testing programs in this book. The *f* indicates that a floating point number is to be printed. In each case, the variable (such as integer, octal, hexadecimal, or float) is named earlier in the program.

The printf line in this program simply tells the machine to print *x*, a decimal integer, on the screen. Each time, the conversion designator must be used to indicate what is to be printed and sometimes how it is to be printed.

Figure 3-8 shows a modified version of the previous program. The only change is the addition of the number 20 between the percent sign and the letter *d*. This indicates that the value of *x* is to be printed on the screen in a space that is at least 20 characters wide. Regardless of what the value of *x* is or becomes, its printing will always occupy a minimum of 20 screen character positions. In this example, the value of *x* is only 5 characters long. Therefore,

```
main()
{
int x;
x=23456;
printf("%20d\n",x);
}
```

Figure 3-8 Modified Version of the Program of Figure 3-7.

when this value is printed on the screen, it will be preceded by 15 spaces. Ergo, the value of *x* has been printed in a space that is a minimum of 20 characters wide, as instructed. If the value of *x* involves more characters than specified in the conversion characters, this is probably of no great importance because the conversion specification simply names the minimum number of character positions and not the maximum.

You may also see conversion specifications given in the following fashion: 1.1f;1.2f;3.2f. These indicate floating point numbers, which are to include a set number of decimal places. The first example indicates a number that will be printed with a minimum of one screen character position and with one digit after the decimal point. The next example allows for two digits after the decimal point, while the third allows for two digits after the decimal and a minimum of three character positions. Again, as of this writing, floating point numbers are not implemented in the SuperSoft C package, but it is my understanding that this will be implemented in future versions.

Referring to the program shown in Figure 3-8, we might wonder just how the character-designation portion of the conversion specification can be used in a practical programming situation. The first thing that comes to mind is printing columns. The first column can begin at position 1 by using a conversion factor of %d, for instance. The next column could end at the twentieth screen position by using %20d. By using variations on this method, we could even perform some limited graphics work using numbers and characters from the machine character set.

Simple Mathematics

At this stage, you probably know enough to start writing some simple mathematics programs in C. This is true even if you've had no previous experience whatsoever with this language and only a modicum of experience in BASIC. To this point, you have learned that variables must be specified by type before they are actually used in an argument. You have also learned that in order to display the value of a variable on the monitor screen, a conversion specification is necessary. When used only to display information at the left-hand side of the screen, the specification consists of a percent sign (%) and a letter that describes the argument (such as decimal or octal). The variable itself is included within the parentheses following the printf function, but outside the quotation marks.

Now, let's do some simple integer math. The program shown in Figure 3-9 simply adds two numbers. The sum is then displayed on the screen. If you examine closely the assignment lines where the variables are given certain values, you will see that these lines are nearly like the lines that would be

```
main()
{
    int x;
    int y;
    int z;
    x=3;
    y=4;
    z=x+y;
    printf("%4d\n",z);
}
```

Figure 3-9   Simple Addition Program in
C Language.

found in a program written in BASIC to accomplish the same thing. Of
course, you would have to remove the semicolons from the *x, y,* and *z* assignment lines, and in some dialects of BASIC, you might have to precede each
line with LET. Take a moment to examine this program carefully and see if
you can identify what is taking place.

Here's how it works on a line-by-line basis. Following the usual main()
and opening brace lines, we see that variables *x, y,* and *z* are defined as integers. The next three lines make the actual assignments. The variable *x* is
equal to 3, *y* is equal to 4, and *z* is equal to the sum of *x* and *y.*

Now, we encounter the printf line. The argument is *z,* because it falls
outside the quotation marks but within the parentheses and is separated
from the previous line entry by a comma. The conversion specification indicates that *z* is to be displayed as a decimal and within a minimum of four
screen character positions. The closing brace in the next line ends the program.

When this program is run, the screen will display the number 7, which
is the sum of 3 and 4. The 7 will be displayed at the fourth character position,
due to the 4*d* designator. If the value of *z* were 7342, the 7 would appear at
the left-hand side of the screen in the first character position, and the 2
would be displayed at the fourth character position. By removing the
number 4 from the printf line in this program, the value of *z* would be
displayed at the first character position on the line. You may substitute other
values for *x* and *y* and for other mathematical operations as well. It is not
necessary to input a screen character number in conversion specifications
unless you desire that the answer be displayed at a point other than at the far
left side of the screen. If you use a line width-specification number and the
value of *z* exceeds this number, no harm is done. The program will run successfully because, again, this number specifies only the *minimum* number of
characters used to display the value.

Simple mathematical operations are handled in C in exactly the same
manner as in most other types of languages. Figure 3-10 shows this same program, which has been set up to first add the values of *x* and *y* and then
multiply the sum by 2. The same printf line is used as before. When the value
of *z* is displayed (14), the number 1 will appear in the third character position
from the left, while the 4 will appear at the fourth position. Again, the con-

14

```
B>type pgmr.c
main()
{
int x;
int y;
int z;
x=3;
y=4;
z=(x+y)*2;
printf("%4d\n",z);
}
```

Figure 3-10 Program That Adds and Then Multiplies Values.

version specification has mandated that a minimum of four screen character positions will be used to display the answer.

C Loops

In learning BASIC, one of the first problems to overcome is to understand what a loop is and then understand the multitude of uses it has. The FOR-NEXT loop is one of the most effective tools of BASIC, and it is simulated quite nicely in most other languages as well.

C is no exception to this, but for the time being, let's forget FOR-NEXT and talk simply about an endless loop. In BASIC, an endless loop might be created by the program line:

100   GOTO 100

This line simply repeats itself over and over again ad infinitum. It is often used in graphics programs written in BASIC to prevent the end-of-execution prompt from appearing on the graphic screen. To demonstrate an endless loop in BASIC, the following program is often used:

10   LET X = 5
20   PRINT X
30   GOTO 20

When this program is run, it produces a continuous series of 5's printed vertically on the screen.

We can accomplish exactly the same thing in C and the GOTO statement is used just as it is in BASIC. The program is shown in Figure 3-11. You can see that the variable *x* is identified as an integer. Following this line is QRP:, which is known as an *identifier*. It is used in conjunction with a goto statement as a marker to indicate where the branch is to be directed. Any type of designation may be used here. I chose QRP at random. I usually

```
main()
{

    int x;

QRP:

    x=5;
    printf("%d\n", x);

    goto QRP;
}
```

Figure 3-11   Use of the goto Statement to Form an Endless Loop in C Language.

capitalize these identifiers to make them plainly visible in larger programs. Whatever you use, make absolutely certain that the identifier is followed by a colon. Otherwise, an error message will occur during the compilation process.

In the next line, the variable x is assigned the value of 5. The following line uses printf to display the value of 5 on the monitor screen. The slash-n portion of the line assures that the cursor will be returned to the left-hand position and the screen line will be advanced each time a printing is completed.

The next line contains the goto statement, which is followed by the identifier previously discussed. In this case, the semicolon follows the identifier. This line tells the computer to branch to the portion of the program immediately following the identifier (QRP). This is the equivalent of GOTO 20 in the BASIC program used as an example. When this program is run, the monitor screen will display a continuous series of 5's at the left-hand side of the screen. Execution has to be halted manually, as this program constitutes an endless, or continuous, loop that will run without stopping.

The endless loop should be quite easy to understand because it works in almost the same manner in C as it does in BASIC, or—for that matter—in most other languages. In C, the FOR-NEXT loop equivalent can be found. However, there is no NEXT. In C, the for statement itself contains all the loop information. In BASIC, FOR and NEXT must surround the operations to be performed. The FOR statement marks the beginning of the loop, while the NEXT statement indicates the cycle ending point. The program shown in Figure 3-12 is a BASIC program designed to print numbers from 1 to 10 on the screen. The C language equivalent is shown in Figure 3-13. Here, variables i, x, and z are identified as integers. The first two are assigned numeric values. The FOR statement is encountered near the bottom of the program, and you should notice immediately that, unlike lines in previous programs, the one containing the FOR statement is not terminated with a

Figure 3-12   Program Written in BASIC to Display the Numbers 1 Through 10 on the Screen.

```
10 FOR X=1 TO 10
20 PRINT X
30 NEXT X
```

```
main()
{
int i;
i=1;
int x;
x=10;
int z;
for(z=i;z<=x;z=z+1)
printf("%1d\n",z);
}
```

Figure 3-13   The C Language Equivalent
of the BASIC Program of Figure 3-13.

semicolon or any symbol at all. For you BASIC language enthusiasts, if you will simply imagine a NEXT statement following the printf line, understanding may be a little easier.

The FOR line tells the machine that the value of z is equal to the value of i. Earlier, i was given a value of 1. Therefore, z equals 1. This is the starting point for the loop. A semicolon separates this assignment from the next. This latter one assigns z a value less than or equal to x. This is the maximum value for z and determines the number of cycles in the loop. Another semicolon is used and z is once again assigned a new value. This one is equivalent to the STEP portion of the FOR statement in BASIC. In this case, z is assigned a value of z plus 1. This simply means that the steps will be in increments of 1. Normally, this would not be written as z plus 1. I have presented it in this manner to conform more closely with what you know about counting methods in BASIC. This expression will execute perfectly in C, but such a counting sequence would normally be written as: $z = + + 1$. In any event, they both have the same meaning.

The printf line immediately follows the for statement line and therefore is inserted within the loop. The semicolon at the end of this line may be thought of as the equivalent of the NEXT statement in BASIC, causing execution to branch back to the for statement line, where the value of z has been incremented by 1. This last statement is not entirely accurate from an actual machine standpoint, but it does convey the basic idea of what is occurring. When the value of z is equal to x or 10, the loop effectively times out and the program is terminated. Figure 3-14 shows the results of the program run.

Please make certain that you understand exactly how the for statement is used in C language. As in BASIC, this statement and the loops it creates are extremely valuable tools that will be used over and over again.

```
1
2
3
4
5
6
7
8
9
10
```

Figure 3-14   Screen Display When Program of Figure 3-13 is Run.

As is the case with all computer languages, there are several ways to accomplish the same thing on the screen or elsewhere. The program just discussed demonstrated the use of the for statement in C language to produce a loop. This program could also be written in a much shorter form by eliminating the variables *i* and *x*. To do this, you would simply remove the first four lines of the program following the opening brace and change the for statement line to:

$$for(z = 1; z < = 10; z = z + 1)$$

Writing the program in this manner makes for an even better comparison of the for statement in C language to the FOR-NEXT loop in BASIC.

A Useful Program in C

So far, all the programs presented have certainly been executable, but they have accomplished little or nothing on other than an instructional level. At this juncture, it is certainly worthwhile to present a program that provides some useful information. Figure 3-15 shows an extremely simple program, which will determine which years in the calendar from 1900 to 2000 are leap years. A leap year is any year that is divisible by 4, but not by 100. This may come as a surprise to many persons, since the majority probably always believed that a leap year was any year evenly divisible by 4. Another way of saying this is that leap year comes every 4 years. This is totally incorrect. The year 1000 was not a leap year because it is evenly divisible by 100. Any year which is evenly divisible by 100 is never a leap year—unless it is evenly divisible by 400. The year 1000 is evenly divisible by 4, so it meets one of the criteria for leap year. However, it is also evenly divisible by 100, which means that it cannot be a leap year unless it is also evenly divisible by 400, which it is not. All of this may come as a surprise to you, but this is officially how leap years are determined.

The program shown in Figure 3-15 indicates which years in the

```
main()
{
int year;
for (year=1900; year<=2000; year=year+1)
if (year % 4 == 0 && year % 100 !=0 || year % 400 ==0)
{
printf("%4d. LEAP YEAR\n",year);
}
}
```

Figure 3-15 Simple Program in C to Detect Leap Years.

100-year period from 1900 to 2000 are leap years. The program uses parts from the programs previously presented in this chapter and also introduces a few more logical operators, which will be discussed later.

The opening two lines of this program contain the main() and the opening brace to indicate the point of execution. A numeric variable is identified as an integer. In this case, I have named the variable *year*. On the next line, the for statement is used to establish a loop. It says: The minimum value is 1900; the maximum value is 2000; the step value is 1.

Surprise! This program utilizes another statement that should be quite familiar to those of you who have even a limited amount of experience in programming in BASIC. The IF statement in BASIC may be followed by THEN, GOSUB, or GOTO and ELSE, depending on the particular dialect. In C, the if statement is used alone and without any other statements or commands. This is similar to the manner in which the for statement is used to establish a loop. You will notice that, like the for statement line, the if statement line does not terminate in a semicolon. You will also notice the addition of another opening brace on the line following the one containing the if statement. The printf line is pretty much standardized by now and does not appear to be significantly altered from its previously discussed uses in this chapter.

The for statement line establishes the loop that counts from 1900 to 2000 in increments of 1. The if statement line falls within the loop. Each time a value of year is determined by the previous line, it is tested within the loop using integer division. Integer division simply truncates any fractional parts. The expression $x \% y$ is an example of integer division. Here, the slash mark is replaced by the percent sign. The solution output from this type of division is the remainder of x divided by y. In other words, the fractional portion is output. If x is evenly divisible by y, the remainder is 0. If x is not evenly divisible by y, the remainder is more than 0. Integer division is used exclusively throughout the if statement line to test the value of year to determine if it is a leap year. In determining a leap year, we are looking for remainders of 0 when integer division is performed with 4 and 400 as divisors. We are looking for a remainder of other than 0 when 100 is used as a divisor.

The if statement line also makes use of equality operators, along with logical operators. The equality operators include = = and ! = . The first simply means equal to and the second means not equal to. The logical operators in this line include && and ¦. The latter symbols may be represented as two solid vertical bars in some character sets. In any event, the first group of symbols indicates the logical AND operation, while the second set is the logical OR operation.

The if statement line says that if the value of the year divided by 4 (integer division) is equal to 0 AND the value of year divided by 100 (integer division) is not equal to 0, OR the value of year divided by 400 (integer division) is equal to 0, then advance on to the printf line. If not, then go through the next cycle of the loop. The following is a BASIC program version of this C program:

```
10   FOR YEAR  =  1900 TO 2000 STEP 1
20   IF YEAR/400  =  INT(YEAR/400) THEN 40
30   IF YEAR/4  =  INT(YEAR/4) AND YEAR/100 < > INT(YEAR/
     400) THEN 40 ELSE 50
40   PRINT YEAR;".LEAP YEAR"
50   NEXT YEAR
```

The printf line is activated in the C program only when all the criteria tested for in the if statement line are true. The open and close braces that surround the printf line indicate that this is the line that is to be executed if the previous line tests true. Comparing the two programs, it is easy to see that writing the C language version is really less time-consuming than writing the BASIC language version because fewer characters need to be input from the keyboard when programming in the former. The output from the program run is shown in Figure 3-16. This output applies to either program.

Let's examine the printf line a little more closely. Near the end of the line and in parentheses is the variable *year,* which is to be substituted for the percent sign at the front of the line. The conversion specification names a decimal integer that is a minimum of 4 screen characters in width, but—at this point—there are a few changes from our previous discussions; more accurately, there is a combining of printf examples. Here, the printf line is used to display the value of a variable on the screen and also to print a string of characters. Anything that appears inside the quotation marks, with the exception of the conversion specification and the slash-n or slash-r, will be printed on the screen. Following the conversion specification and preceding the backslash is the string . LEAP YEAR. This string will be printed on the screen after the value of the variable is printed. The printout in Figure 3-16 shows that the value of the variable *year* is printed first. It is immediately

```
                         1904.  LEAP  YEAR
                         1908.  LEAP  YEAR
                         1912.  LEAP  YEAR
                         1916.  LEAP  YEAR
                         1920.  LEAP  YEAR
                         1924.  LEAP  YEAR
                         1928.  LEAP  YEAR
                         1932.  LEAP  YEAR
                         1936.  LEAP  YEAR
**Figure 3-16**   Sample Program Run Using    1940.  LEAP  YEAR
Program of Figure 3-15.                       1944.  LEAP  YEAR
```

followed by the period (.), a space, and then the words LEAP YEAR. This provides for an appealing and easy-to-read screen display.

As before, you can write this program in many different ways. Variables can be assigned values that correspond to the high and low values of year in the for statement line. However, this sometimes leads to difficulty in understanding a program. Fortunately, C language is equipped with methods of defining names or constants symbolically at the beginning of a program and before execution actually begins. One method involves using # define. This construction is used to define a name as a particular string of characters. Anytime this name is encountered within the executable portion of the program, it is replaced by the corresponding string. This occurs during the compilation process.

Figure 3-17 shows the leap year program discussed earlier, but this version makes use of # define. Here, LOW is equal to 1900, HIGH is equal to 2000, and STEP is equal to 1. This tells you something about the program, because LOW, HIGH, and STEP are used in the for statement line. LOW is the lowest value for variable *year*. HIGH is the highest value this variable may assume. STEP names the increments by which the variable is counted from 1900 to 2000. The # define constructions are placed before main() in this program. The executable portion of the program occurs after main(). The # define constructions are used during the compilation process. In the actual version of the program that is run by your machine, the for statement line is:

$$\text{for (year} = 1900; \text{year} < = 2000; \text{year} = \text{year} + 1)$$

This is exactly the way this line appears in the first program used to calculate leap year. The second version, which includes the # define construction, will tell you more about the program than the first one when both programs are displayed on a line-by-line basis. Again, from an execution standpoint, both

```
B>type pgmr.c
#define  LOW   1900
#define  HIGH  2000
#define  STEP  1
main()
{
int year;
for (year=LOW; year<=HIGH; year=year+STEP)
if (year % 4 == 0 && year % 100 !=0 !! year % 400 ==0)
{
printf("%4d. LEAP YEAR\n",year);
}
}
```

Figure 3–17   Different Version of the Leap Year Program.

programs appear to be identical to the computer. The difference lies in ease of understanding for the programmer.

Counting Routines

In many programs written in any language, it is often necessary to build in a count routine, which indicates the number of times a subroutine is accessed. When a count routine is entered into the body of a program, it usually assigns a value to a numeric variable that increases in various steps (usually 1) each time that line is executed. When the value of the numeric variable reaches a certain point, a branch may occur or the program may be terminated.

The following sample program in BASIC illustrates a counting routine:

```
10   FOR X  =  1 TO 100 STEP 1
20   IF X/2  =  INT(X/2) THEN 30 ELSE 40
30   I = I + 1
40   IF I = 40 THEN END
50   NEXT X
```

In this example, a FOR-NEXT loop is established that counts from 1 to 100 in steps of 1. In line 20, a test is made to see if the value of X is divisible by 2. If it is, there is a branch to line 30, which contains the counting routine. Here, the variable I is equal to itself plus 1. The first time line 30 is accessed, I will be equal to 0 plus 1. The second time it is encountered, it will be equal to 1 plus 1, or 2; the third time, it will be equal to 2 plus 1, or 3, and so on. If the value of X divided by 2 is not equal to the integer value of X divided by 2 (X is not evenly divisible by 2), there is a branch to line 40. Notice that line 30 is bypassed in the execution. Line 40 is a test line that creates a branch when the value of the count variable I is equal to 40. At this point, the program is terminated.

The following program shows another example of a count line being used in a BASIC program:

```
10   X = X + 1
20   PRINT X;
30   GOTO 10
```

This program is on an endless loop and will print the value of X horizontally on the screen. Theoretically, the program will never end because line 30 always branches back to the beginning, so the value of X continues to increase until the program is manually halted. This program simply demonstrates how a counting line works.

The program shown in Figure 3-18 is the C language version of this BASIC program. After main() and the opening brace, the variable x is identified as an integer (int x;). In the next line, x is assigned a value of 1. The beginning of a continuous loop is established in the next line with the identifier QRP:. The printf line indicates that the variable x is to be printed as a decimal integer; in the following line, x is reassigned the value x plus 1. However, it is customary to write this as $+ + x$ when programming in C. The goto statement line branches to the portion of the program immediately following the identifier QRP:. The line that initially assigns a value of 1 to x lies outside the loop. Therefore, it is executed once and only once. From that point on, the reassignment line (x = + + x;) determines the value of x.

```
main()
{
int x;
x=1;
QRP:
printf("%d;",x);
x=++x;
goto QRP;
}
```

Figure 3-18 Counting Program in C Language.

Let's discuss the printf line a bit further. You will notice what might appear to be an omission. There is no slash-n return character. This was purposely omitted in an effort to duplicate the output display produced by the BASIC program used as an example. You will remember that this program printed the value of X horizontally on the screen due to the PRINT X; statement. (The semicolon following the X indicates a horizontal rather than vertical format.)

When programming in C, the slash-n designation found within a printf line acts as a carriage return, or more appropriately, a cursor return and line advance. When this is omitted, all printed items appear horizontally. Naturally, the computer itself will reverse carriage when the printed information runs off the right side of the screen. The printf line also contains a semicolon within quotation marks. Therefore, the screen will display the value of x, followed by a semicolon. Figure 3-19 shows a portion of the program run. It was manually halted after x had stepped to a value of 192. Without the semicolon used as a separator, all these numbers would run together. You can see that there is not much difference in setting up a counting routine in C as opposed to accomplishing the same thing in BASIC once a few facts about the former are known.

```
B>pgmr
MSDOS Run time V1.2.29  Copyright 1983 SuperSoft
1;2;3;4;5;6;7;8;9;10;11;12;13;14;15;16;17;18;19;20;21;22;23;24;25;26;27;28;29;30
;31;32;33;34;35;36;37;38;39;40;41;42;43;44;45;46;47;48;49;50;51;52;53;54;55;56;5
7;58;59;60;61;62;63;64;65;66;67;68;69;70;71;72;73;74;75;76;77;78;79;80;81;82;83;
84;85;86;87;88;89;90;91;92;93;94;95;96;97;98;99;100;101;102;103;104;105;106;107;
108;109;110;111;112;113;114;115;116;117;118;119;120;121;122;123;124;125;126;127;
128;129;130;131;132;133;134;135;136;137;138;139;140;141;142;143;144;145;146;147;
148;149;150;151;152;153;154;155;156;157;158;159;160;161;162;163;164;165;166;167;
168;169;170;171;172;173;174;175;176;177;178;179;180;181;182;183;184;185;186;187;
188;189;190;191;192;
```

Figure 3-19 Program Run From Previous Program.

Summary

In this chapter, a few of the more important functions and statements in C language are discussed and used in working programs. While there are many more functions and statements to be considered and explored in detail, it is absolutely mandatory that you understand what has already been presented in order to move further in this study. Before moving on to the next chapter, it is highly recommended that you reread any portion of this chapter that you do not understand fully. Most of the functions, statements, and programming techniques presented in this chapter are used again and again in following chapters. This method of teaching the basics of a new language involves concentration on an extremely limited number of statements and functions at the onset, expanding upon their uses, and adding more functions and statements as we become more proficient.

In order to test your proficiency in what has already been presented, consider the following assignment and write a program to accomplish each in C language.

1. Create a program to subtract the number 201 from the number 473.
2. Using a loop, create a program that will subtract the numbers 10 through 200 in steps of 10 from 240 through 440.
3. Create a program to count from 1 to 400 in steps of 1 but to print MARK when the number 100 is reached. (*Hint:* Remember the if statement.)
4. Create a program that will print your name ten times on the screen in a vertical format and with double spacing between printed lines. (*Hint:* Slash-n in printf function line will create a single line advance. What would slash-n followed by another slash-n accomplish?)
5. Create a program that will add the numbers 14 and 23 and then multiply the sum by a series of numbers of from 2 to 30 in steps of 1.

Each of these assignments is quite simple, but each will give you the opportunity to practice programming on your own in C language. A few will require a bit of intuitive guesswork on your part as well. The programs that will meet these assignments are not given in another portion of this text. Indeed, there are hundreds of different programs that can be used to fulfill any one. By perusing the information contained in this chapter, you should be able to create the programs assigned. If not, reread this chapter and make certain you understand its content before moving further. To do otherwise will further retard your progress in learning C.

Before leaving this chapter, we observe that the method we have used for displaying program line listings to this point is considered to be quite unorthodox among C programmers. You have probably seen other C programs and noticed that, for the most part, only a few lines contain functions, definitions, or statements that are printed at the far left-hand side. The following demonstrates the proper method (according to most programmers) for presenting one of the C programs discussed earlier in this chapter.

```
main( )
{
        printf("hello, how are you \ n");
}
```

The opening main ( ) is typed at the left side of the screen, as is the opening brace. All other lines are usually indented to a point falling in the same character block as the right parentheses in main ( ). If you use an if statement, it is usually appropriate to indent the instruction that immediately follows to a point falling beneath the open parenthesis following this statement. The same applies to the executed loop lines following a FOR statement.

This type of program follows the formats common to many other types of computer languages. However, BASIC is not one of them. From an execution standpoint, it makes little difference how much white space you use. In this first chapter, all lines begin at the extreme left-hand margin to create less confusion for those of you who are just beginning to explore C. I have found that one of the most disturbing aspects of a new language in regard to how it is used by students with experience only in BASIC is the lack of a program line number and what appear to be foreign statements, commands, and functions spread all over the screen. Such students seem to feel that if you don't provide some exact number of blanks (white spaces) preceding a statement line, an error message will be generated. Many C programmers will provide spaces between variables and operators, as in:

$$x = y$$

This will work just as well in C if you use:

$$x = y$$

There may be exceptions to this, but I have not heard of them and I find that the SuperSoft package and my machine seem to be quite versatile and, indeed, forgiving, of random white-space separators at some points and not at others. The same is true in most dialects of BASIC. We continue with this format throughout most of the next chapter, but we eventually make the switch to an appropriate C format. The reason for the multitude of white spaces used by most C programmers is to provide clarity of understanding to those who read the program lines and possibly write other programs from these concepts. Once you get used to the difference in formats between BASIC and C, you should be able to realize fully the clarity advantage this latter format offers.

4 INPUT CONTROL PROGRAMS

The previous chapter outlined some basic programming methods using C programming language and allowed mathematical operations to take place by inserting the various values directly in the function argument or by substituting assigned variables to accomplish the same task. Such programs are useful for demonstration purposes and it is to be hoped that they have gone a long way toward allowing you to understand some of the basic programming operations of this fascinating computer language.

From a standpoint of practicality, however, most programs that perform a clearly identified mathematical operation(s) are really set electronic formulas into which the user can input the variables that are to be acted upon. This means that the user must be able to input characters via some external device. In most instances, this is the keyboard.

In BASIC, there are several statements that allow for keyboard input to be inserted into various portions of the running program. The INPUT statement is probably the most common. This statement halts program execution until some input is obtained from the keyboard. Execution continues when Enter is pressed. Several other functions and/or statements will allow for other types of input information as well. One of these is INKEY$, which (when used properly within a program) can be used to set up a locked loop until any key on the active keyboard is pressed. When this occurs, the locked loop is broken, and execution continues. It is also possible to use INKEY$ with proper IF-THEN statements to branch to another program portion (outside of the locked loop) when a specific key is depressed.

The INPUT statement may be used to allow for string information to be input via the keyboard. This can include words, phrases, and/or numbers and might read: INPUT A$. On the other hand, a numeric variable may be specified, which means that only numeric numbers are acceptable. The equivalent of this would be: INPUT A.

In C programming language, each of these statements has an equivalent function, although there are distinct differences in some of them. However, the differences are great enough to stop you from making very satisfactory comparisons and indeed using the C function equivalents to take their places in a C program. I am still assuming that you are thinking in terms of BASIC while writing programs, regardless of what language is being used at the time. In other words, you visualize a programming concept and then mentally define a method of accomplishing this goal using BASIC. You then make the necessary mental conversions to C and proceed from there to write the program in C. As your proficiency with C increases, you will go through this translation process less and less. However, for the time being, such a process is neither unusual nor undesirable. If you can see how this new language (C) relates to a language you know well (BASIC), a fuller understanding of both languages is easily obtained.

This chapter presents many of the functions found in C that allow for direct input via the keyboard. As was the case in the previous chapter, each one of these functions is presented in terms of simple programs that you may input directly to your machine, compile, and run. You see firsthand what each programming step accomplishes and, undoubtedly, you see what effect typing errors have on the compiler run and the error messages they generate. Fortunately, if you make a typing error during the writing process, the SuperSoft C compiler will usually print an error message and a line listing of where these errors occur immediately after the first pass is completed. This will give you the opportunity to stop the compilation process near the beginning and then return to your line editor in order to correct the programming mistakes before attempting compilation again. Setting up the compiler in a similar manner to that described in Chapter 2 allows for fast compilation time, so you can see the results of your program while each line is fresh in your mind.

getchar

In C, getchar is used to return the next character from the keyboard. The input device may be something other than a keyboard, but for the sake of all discussions in this chapter, we assume the keyboard is the only input device. Comparing C with BASIC, getchar is closely equivalent to the INKEY$ variable. The following program in BASIC demonstrates a typical use of IN-KEY$.

```
10   A$ = INKEY$
20   IF A$ = "" THEN 10 ELSE 30
30   END
```

This program establishes an endless loop between lines 10 and 20 as long as no key is pressed. Execution is not halted, as would be the case with an IN-PUT statement. Line 10 is executed and then line 20 is executed. If there is no keyboard input, line 20 branches to line 10, and the process begins again. The INKEY$ variable causes the machine to read the keyboard. The value of any key that is pressed is assigned to the string variable A$. The test line in program line 20 states simply that if the value of A$ is equal to a null input (""), branch to line 10. If the value of A$ is equal to anything other than a null input, branch to line 30. The back-to-back quotation marks indicate that only a null input will send the execution back to line 10.

INKEY$ is neither a statement nor a function in itself. Rather, it is a variable incorporated like other variables (string and numeric) in a BASIC program. This might accurately be called a specialized function variable, but, in the long run, all it does is assign to a string variable a value equal to the keyboard input.

The C language function getchar, while comparable to INKEY$, is actually far more powerful. It is a true function in itself and, when used in a program, execution stops until any character from the keyboard is received. The C program equivalent to the BASIC program just presented would be:

```
main( )
{
getchar( );
}
```

When this program is run, execution will halt until any character from the keyboard is typed in. At this point, the program will end. Notice that neither the BASIC version nor the program written in C produces any on-screen information. The getchar function may be used in this manner to bring about a temporary halt in program execution in order to give the operator time to absorb the information that has been printed previously and assimilate needed input information for future use. This type of use is very reminiscent of the INPUT statement in BASIC for the same purposes. A statement such as INPUT A$ may be placed anywhere within a BASIC program to bring about a temporary program halt. The keyboard information input for A$ is not important in this type of use. What is important is that the program has been halted, but execution can be started again by simply pressing Enter. This differs from the INKEY$ program discussed earlier, which allows execution to continue outside of the locked loop when any key is pressed. When INPUT A$ is used, program execution is halted and will not begin again until the Enter key is pressed. Again, when getchar is used as shown in the previous example, it may be thought of as a self-contained continuous loop like one that might be created with the INKEY$ program, although getchar(); is all that is required to halt execution until any key is pressed. When the latter occurs, the remaining lines in the C program will be executed.

The C function getchar differs from both INPUT and INKEY$ in that it does not actually return the character of the key pressed, but rather, the ASCII code for that character. This is unimportant when getchar is used as shown previously. However, it becomes extremely important when getchar is used in another manner. This is demonstrated by the following program:

```
main( )
{
int i;
i= getchar( );
printf("2d \ n",x);
}
```

int x;
x = getchar( );

— correction: J. Schilling 8505.25

Here, getchar is used as a combination of INPUT A$ and INKEY$. As soon as the getchar line is reached, execution is effectively halted until any key is pressed. When this occurs, as before, execution continues; at the same time, the ASCII value of the character that has been input is assigned to the integer variable *x*. The printf line uses familiar terminology to display the value of *x* on the screen. Whenever you press a key, its ASCII code will appear immediately thereafter. When the program is run, its execution will wait for the keyboard input. The program will not terminate its run until the key has been pressed and its ASCII code printed. You can type any character you wish (letter or numeral), but you can type only one. As soon as the first key is pressed, execution is immediately started again and the keyboard read function is eliminated.

The getchar function returns the ASCII *code* of any key on the keyboard. This is completely different from the BASIC statement INPUT, which returns the keyboard character rather than the ASCII *code*. This is the same as INKEY$. Certainly, there are persons who will argue with my terminology here, in that in BASIC programming, the ASCII *code* is always returned whenever we deal with the keyboard or computer input/output in general. From a teaching standpoint, however, it is safe to say that for all intents and purposes, INPUT and INKEY$ in BASIC *seem* to return the keyboard character, whereas in C programming language, the ASCII code is returned.

To many, this might seem to be a limitation, and in some ways it is if you need to read an actual keyboard character and display it on the screen. However, there are many easy ways this ASCII code character can be converted to an actual keyboard character. There are also other functions in C that can return keyboard characters rather than the ASCII code for each.

Figure 4-1 shows a more complex program that uses getchar and many of the other statements discussed in Chapter 3. It also introduces a new function that is used to terminate a program run permanently. This is the exit

```
main()
{
int i;
int x;
QRP:
x=getchar();
if(x==88) {
printf("THE PROGRAM IS TERMINATED!!\n");
exit(i);
}
printf("STRIKE ANY KEY (EXCEPT 'X') TO CONTINUE PROGRAM RUN.\n");
printf("STRIKE THE UPPER CASE (X) KEY TO END PROGRAM.\n");
printf("PROGRAM RUNNING!\n");
goto QRP;
}
```

Figure 4-1   Program Demonstrating the getchar Function.

function which, for the time being, may be thought of as the equivalent of the END statement in BASIC. The format for the exit function is:

exit(i);

In this case, variable *i* is a dummy argument. In future versions of this compiler, the variable may be implemented to transfer control to another system or even to load and run another program. In present implementation, the variable used within the parentheses must be defined as an integer.

Looking at the program on a line-by-line basis, you can see that the two variables *i* and *x* are defined as integers. The QRP: identifier should indicate that this program includes the possibility of a branch to this point. The variable *x* is assigned the ASCII code value of whatever key is pressed when this line has been executed. An if statement is used in the next line to test for a needed value. Notice that an equality operator (= =) has been used to match variable *x* with the value of 88. This is the equivalent of:

IF X = 88 THEN (branch)

in BASIC.

This line tests for a condition whereby the character returned by getchar to variable *x* is equal to ASCII code 88. This represents the capital letter *X*. You will also notice an opening brace symbol on the same line on which the if statement appears. This is certainly permitted in C programming, but the opening brace could just as easily have been placed on the next line. This brace indicates that the functions following it will be carried out if the condition is true (*x* being equal to 88). The next line will display a program termination message on the screen, but only if *x* is equal to 88. The line after that contains the exit function, which means the program execution will be terminated here, but only if *x* is equal to 88. The next line contains the closing brace. This marks the end of the functions that will be activated if *x* is equal to 88.

The next three printf lines are designed to provide user prompts. The first line tells the user to strike any key except *X* to continue the program run. The next line displays the message that tells the operator to strike the upper-case *X* to end the program. The printf line after that indicates that the program is running. You will notice that each of the printf lines is terminated inside quotation marks with a slash-n newline character. The following statement line branches to the QRP: identifier.

The program works in the following manner. When the run is first started, execution halts at the getchar function. When you press any key on the keyboard (other than capital *X*), you will get the equivalent of this program's menu, telling you what to do to continue the program run and what to do to terminate it. As soon as these messages appear, the goto branch brings execution back to the getchar function, and you have the option of running it again by typing any character except capital *X* or terminating it with the capital *X*. The ASCII code for capital *X* is 88. As long as the input character is not equal to ASCII 88, the printf program termination line and the exit line are not executed. However, when you press capital *X,* the program termination line is executed, and the program is terminated. Figure 4-2 shows a sample run. Notice that the triggering keyboard input is displayed at the far left side of the opening menu message. In the last line, you can see that a capital *X* was input to trigger the termination sequence.

```
PROGRAM RUNNING!
RSTRIKE ANY KEY (EXCEPT 'X') TO CONTINUE PROGRAM RUN.
STRIKE THE UPPER CASE (X) KEY TO END PROGRAM.
PROGRAM RUNNING!
RSTRIKE ANY KEY (EXCEPT 'X') TO CONTINUE PROGRAM RUN.
STRIKE THE UPPER CASE (X) KEY TO END PROGRAM.
PROGRAM RUNNING!
RSTRIKE ANY KEY (EXCEPT 'X') TO CONTINUE PROGRAM RUN.
STRIKE THE UPPER CASE (X) KEY TO END PROGRAM.
PROGRAM RUNNING!
RSTRIKE ANY KEY (EXCEPT 'X') TO CONTINUE PROGRAM RUN.
STRIKE THE UPPER CASE (X) KEY TO END PROGRAM.
PROGRAM RUNNING!
RSTRIKE ANY KEY (EXCEPT 'X') TO CONTINUE PROGRAM RUN.
STRIKE THE UPPER CASE (X) KEY TO END PROGRAM.
PROGRAM RUNNING!
RSTRIKE ANY KEY (EXCEPT 'X') TO CONTINUE PROGRAM RUN.
STRIKE THE UPPER CASE (X) KEY TO END PROGRAM.
PROGRAM RUNNING!
RSTRIKE ANY KEY (EXCEPT 'X') TO CONTINUE PROGRAM RUN.
STRIKE THE UPPER CASE (X) KEY TO END PROGRAM.
PROGRAM RUNNING!
XTHE PROGRAM IS TERMINATED!!
```

Figure 4-2 Sample Program Run.

This program effectively demonstrates the use of several different C functions and statements. You should be able to see how getchar temporarily halts program execution, reads the keyboard, and is used to make assignments to variables. You can also see how the exit function is used to stop program execution permanently.

From the standpoint of clarity, the program run leaves a bit to be desired, however, in that the menu and the triggering letters all seem to run together. This can be corrected by slight alterations to the printf lines or by the addition of another one. The program shown in Figure 4-3 has added a printf line that contains only a newline command. Each time a character is input at getchar, the next executed line is this new one, which simply advances one line on the screen. This means that the menu messages will be printed below the line on which your input key character has appeared. The new program run is shown in Figure 4-4. This one is certainly easier to read

```
main()
{
int i;
int x;
QRP:
x=getchar();
printf("\n");
if(x==88)  {
printf("THE PROGRAM IS TERMINATED!!\n");
exit(i);
}
printf("STRIKE ANY KEY (EXCEPT 'X') TO CONTINUE PROGRAM RUN.\n");
printf("STRIKE THE UPPER CASE (X) KEY TO END PROGRAM.\n");
printf("PROGRAM RUNNING!\n");
goto QRP;
}
```

Figure 4–3   Modified Version of Program in Figure 4–2.

than the previous one and required only a few seconds of additional programming time. Even during the stages of learning a new language, concentrating on clearly presenting the screen output from your program is very important. This will pay off as your proficiency increases.

The program shown in Figure 4-5 demonstrates another use of getchar.
This is similar to the first use discussed, where a comparison was made with
the INKEY$ variable in BASIC. There's nothing highly unusual about the
program, but you will notice that the printf line contains double slash-n combinations. This is the answer to one of the assignment problems given in
Chapter 3. Whereas a slash-n will produce a single new line, two of them will
produce two new lines, or the computer equivalent of a double space. When
this program is run, nothing will happen until you press any key. When this

```
I
STRIKE ANY KEY (EXCEPT 'X') TO CONTINUE PROGRAM RUN.
STRIKE THE UPPER CASE (X) KEY TO END PROGRAM.
PROGRAM RUNNING!
O
STRIKE ANY KEY (EXCEPT 'X') TO CONTINUE PROGRAM RUN.
STRIKE THE UPPER CASE (X) KEY TO END PROGRAM.
PROGRAM RUNNING!
P
STRIKE ANY KEY (EXCEPT 'X') TO CONTINUE PROGRAM RUN.
STRIKE THE UPPER CASE (X) KEY TO END PROGRAM.
PROGRAM RUNNING!
L
STRIKE ANY KEY (EXCEPT 'X') TO CONTINUE PROGRAM RUN.
STRIKE THE UPPER CASE (X) KEY TO END PROGRAM.
PROGRAM RUNNING!
K
STRIKE ANY KEY (EXCEPT 'X') TO CONTINUE PROGRAM RUN.
STRIKE THE UPPER CASE (X) KEY TO END PROGRAM.
PROGRAM RUNNING!
X
THE PROGRAM IS TERMINATED!!
```

Figure 4–4   Modified Program Run.

```
main()
{
QRP:
getchar();
printf("MR. ROBERT J. TRAISTER\n\n")
goto QRP;
}
```

Figure 4-5 A Program Using getchar to
Halt Execution Temporarily Until Any
Key is Pressed.

occurs, the quoted line in the printf function is displayed on the screen, followed by two newline characters. There is then a branch to getchar, and
pressing any other key will cause the phrase to be printed again. The resulting
display is shown in Figure 4-6. This is another method which can be used to
assure a clear and concise on-screen presentation.

```
MR. ROBERT J. TRAISTER

MR. ROBERT J. TRAISTER

MR. ROBERT J. TRAISTER

MR. ROBERT J. TRAISTER
```

Figure 4-6 Program Run in Which a
Keyboard Key Was Pressed Four Different Times.

The getchar function is very valuable in writing programs which allow
the user to input mathematical quantities to be acted upon by a formula
within the program. One version of such a program is shown in Figure 4-7.
This one does not use getchar, but assigns the variable within the program.
In this example, 300 is substituted for x. The variable z contains the
mathematical formula into which x is worked. The printf line displays the
answer in the minimum space of four screen characters.

```
main()
{
int x;
int z;
x=300;
z=((x-32)*5)/9;
printf("%4d\n",z);
}
```

Figure 4-7 Program Using a Fixed
Quantity of x to Be Worked into a
Mathematical Formula.

Figure 4-8 shows the keyboard input equivalent of this program. You
will notice that only one line has been altered. Here, x is equal to the ASCII
character equivalent. If you type capital X, the value of 88 will be inserted
into the formula.

```
main()
{
int x;
int z;
x=getchar();
z=((x-32)*5)/9;
printf("%4d\n",z);
}
```

Figure 4-8 Modification of the Program
of Figure 4-7 Using getchar to Input
ASCII Values From Keyboard.

```
main()
{
int c;
int x;
x=1;
QRP:
printf("%1d;",x);
if (x==340) {
printf("\n");
printf("x=340:PROGRAM HALTED::PRESS ENTER TO CONTINUE SEQUENCE\n");
printf("OR, PRESS 'X' TO RESTART SEQUENCE.\n");
c=getchar();
}
if(c==88) {
x=0;
c=1;
}
x=++x;
goto QRP;
}
```

Figure 4-9 Expanded Version of the Program of Figure 4-8.

Figure 4-9 shows another example of the use of getchar. The use is the same as before, but the program has been expanded using two if statements. Here, variables c and x are identified as integers, and x is tentatively assigned a value of 1. The identifier QRP: marks the repetition or branch point. The next line prints the value of x on the screen. The test lines follow, which eventually create branches, depending on the value of x. This is a counting routine, and x will be stepped in increments of 1 during each cycle of the loop. The first if statement activates the next four lines when x is equal to 340. If x has not been counted to 340, there is an effective branch near the bottom of this program and the line reading x = + +x;. The goto statement then branches to the identifier QRP: and x is stepped again. When 340 passes have been made, the first if statement argument proves true and the four program lines within the opening and closing braces are executed. Here, the operator is informed that x is equal to 340 and that the program is halted. At this point, the Enter key, or for that matter, any other key except capital X, may be pressed to continue the sequence. This means that the count will resume at 341. However, if a capital X is pressed, the sequence starts at the beginning again. Notice the getchar function following the last printf line. This reads the input from the keyboard. Below the closing brace is another if statement, which checks for a value of ASCII 88 (capital X). If this key is pressed, variable x is reassigned the value of 0 and c is reassigned a value of 1. This effectively resets the count sequence to 0. The variable c is assigned any number but 88. This acts as a reset as well.

The count routine is once again entered, along with the branches, and the count will again rise to 340 before the program is temporarily halted. Figure 4-10 shows a portion of a program run. The top portion shows the last part of the count to 340, followed by the instructions for continuance. In this example, the capital X was input to restart the sequence at 1. Figure 4-11

```
;268;269;270;271;272;273;274;275;276;277;278;279;280;281;282;283;284;285;286;287
;288;289;290;291;292;293;294;295;296;297;298;299;300;301;302;303;304;305;306;307
;308;309;310;311;312;313;314;315;316;317;318;319;320;321;322;323;324;325;326;327
;328;329;330;331;332;333;334;335;336;337;338;339;340;
x=340:PROGRAM HALTED::PRESS ENTER TO CONTINUE SEQUENCE
OR, PRESS 'X' TO RESTART SEQUENCE.
X1;2;3;4;5;6;7;8;9;10;11;12;13;14;15;16;17;18;19;20;21;22;23;24;25;26;27;28;29;3
0;31;32;33;34;35;36;37;38;39;40;41;42;43;44;45;46;47;48;49;50;51;52;53;54;55;56;
57;58;59;60;61;62;63;64;65;66;67;68;69;70;71;72;73;74;75;76;77;78;79;80;81;82;83
;84;85;86;87;88;89;90;91;92;93;94;95;96;97;98;99;100;101;102;103;104;105;106;107
;108;109;110;111;112;113;114;115;116;117;118;119;120;121;122;123;124;125;126;127
;128;129;130;131;132;133;134;135;136;137;138;139;140;141;142;143;144;145;146;147
;148;149;150;151;152;153;154;155;156;157;158;159;160;161;162;163;164;165;166;167
;168;169;170;171;172;173;174;175;176;177;178;179;180;181;182;183;184;185;186;187
;188;189;190;191;192;193;194;195;196;197;198;199;200;201;202;203;204;205;206;207
;208;209;210;211;212;213;214;215;216;217;218;219;220;221;222;223;224;225;226;227
;228;229;230;231;232;233;234;235;236;237;238;239;240;241;242;243;244;245;246;247
;248;249;250;251;252;253;254;255;256;257;258;259;260;261;262;263;264;265;266;267
;268;269;270;271;272;273;274;275;276;277;278;279;280;281;282;283;284;285;286;287
;288;289;290;291;292;293;294;295;296;297;298;299;300;301;302;303;304;305;306;307
;308;309;310;311;312;313;314;315;316;317;318;319;320;321;322;323;324;325;326;327
;328;329;330;331;332;333;334;335;336;337;338;339;340;
x=340:PROGRAM HALTED::PRESS ENTER TO CONTINUE SEQUENCE
OR, PRESS 'X' TO RESTART SEQUENCE.
```

Figure 4-10   Program Run of the Program of Figure 4-8.

```
248;249;250;251;252;253;254;255;256;257;258;259;260;261;262;263;264;265;266;267;
268;269;270;271;272;273;274;275;276;277;278;279;280;281;282;283;284;285;286;287;
288;289;290;291;292;293;294;295;296;297;298;299;300;301;302;303;304;305;306;307;
308;309;310;311;312;313;314;315;316;317;318;319;320;321;322;323;324;325;326;327;
328;329;330;331;332;333;334;335;336;337;338;339;340;
x=340:PROGRAM HALTED::PRESS ENTER TO CONTINUE SEQUENCE
OR, PRESS 'X' TO RESTART SEQUENCE.
341;342;343;344;345;346;347;348;349;350;351;352;353;354;355;356;357;358;359;360
;361;362;363;364;365;366;367;368;369;370;371;372;373;374;375;376;377;378;379;380
;381;382;383;384;385;386;387;388;389;390;391;392;393;394;395;396;397;398;399;400
;401;402;403;404;405;406;407;408;409;410;411;412;413;414;415;416;417;418;419;420
;421;422;423;424;425;426;427;428;429;430;431;432;433;434;435;436;437;438;439;440
;441;442;443;444;445;446;447;448;449;450;451;452;453;454;455;456;457;458;459;460
;461;462;463;464;465;466;467;468;469;470;471;472;473;474;475;476;477;478;479;480
;481;482;483;484;485;486;487;488;489;490;491;492;493;494;495;496;497;498;499;500
;501;502;503;504;505;506;507;508;509;510;511;512;513;514;515;516;517;518;519;520
;521;522;523;524;525;526;527;528;529;530;531;532;533;534;535;536;537;538;539;540
;541;542;543;544;545;546;547;548;549;550;551;552;553;554;555;556;557;558;559;560
;561;562;563;564;565;566;567;568;569;570;571;572;573;574;575;576;577;578;579;580
;581;582;583;584;585;586;587;588;589;590;591;592;593;594;595;596;597;598;599;600
;601;602;603;604;605;606;607;608;
```

Figure 4-11 Another Program Run.

shows another program run. Here, Enter was pressed, and you can see that the count continues from 341. Each number is separated by a semicolon due to the insertion of this character in the first printf line.

While getchar may be used in the format

getchar( )

to serve as a temporary program halt until a key is pressed on the keyboard, it is almost never used in this manner. While an example was shown previously to make a comparison between this function and its equivalent in BASIC, you will almost always see getchar used in the format of:

x = getchar( )

Getchar is specifically used to return a character from the keyboard. However, there is another function common to SuperSoft C that can be used to bring about a temporary program halt until any key is pressed. It behaves very much like the getchar function, except the key character is not displayed on the screen. This is called the *pause function* and it suspends execution of the current program until a character is typed from the console keyboard. Like the INKEY$ variable, pause executes a null loop while testing whether input is present at the keyboard. This null loop is exited and control is returned to the program when a character is input. Figure 4-12 shows an example of the use of pause in a simple program. Here, the integer y is assigned a value of 27, and the pause line is then executed. The program halts at this point (effectively) until you press any key on the keyboard. At this time, the printf line is executed and the numeric value of y is displayed. Regardless of which key you press to return control to the main body of the program, this character will not appear on the screen.

```
main()
{
int y;
y=27;
pause();
printf("%d\n",y);
}
```

Figure 4-12   Program that Demonstrates the pause Function.

scanf

A highly useful function in C is scanf. It is partially equivalent to an INPUT statement in BASIC, which allows for multiple strings or numeric values, as in:

INPUT A,B,C

It also behaves like the INKEY$ variable, meaning that as soon as the input requirements are met, program execution continues. It is not necessary to reinstitute execution by pressing the Enter key.

The scanf function reads a formatted input string from the keyboard. Any book or manual that you read about C describes this function in great detail because it is capable of doing many different things. However, such explanations can be difficult to understand without some specific programming examples.

Figure 4-13 shows our sample program. If you understand how this program works, your understanding of the scanf function will be increased a hundredfold. First, you should think of scanf as the reciprocal of printf. The latter function is used to display formatted information on the screen. The scanf function is designed to pull information from the keyboard following a specific format. This does not necessarily mean that the input information need be in a special format, only that the scanf function will take a relatively random input from the keyboard and place this information in a preassigned format.

```
main()
{
int i;
int x;
scanf("%4d %4d",&i,&x);
printf("\n\n");
printf("%d %d",i,x);
}
```

Figure 4-13   Program Demonstrating the scanf Function.

In this program, variables *i* and *x* are identified as integers. The scanf line specifies the following:

%4d   This portion indicates that the first four digits from the keyboard are decimal integers.

%4d   This second and identical portion indicates the next four digits from the keyboard are decimal integers.

&i   This is an argument called a *pointer* due to the use of the ampersand. The variable *i* is assigned the value of the first four input digits.

&x   This is another argument assigned to the second %4d conversion sequence.

The first %4d value is assigned to *i,* while the second is assigned to *x.* This program demonstrates the scanf use by following this line with a printf line. This particular line simply double-spaces between the input and the next printf line, which displays the values of the input to scanf. The last printf line uses conversion sequences and variable arguments *i* and *x.*

This program is looking for eight decimal characters to be input via the keyboard. As soon as eight characters are typed in, scanf literally shuts down and will accept no further input. The first four characters input are assigned to variable *i*. The next four are assigned to variable *x*. If you input:

12345678

as soon as you input the 8, scanf shuts down. The variable *i* is now equal to 1234, while *x* is equal to 5678. The last printf line will display their values as:

1234   5678

Now, scanf, while waiting for eight decimal integers from the keyboard, will shut down immediately if it receives an input that is not a decimal integer. (Spaces are counted as null characters and have no effect.) Therefore, if you input

1234H

the printout is:

1234   0

The letter *H* is not a decimal integer. Therefore, scanf assumes that its *proper* input string is ended and the shutdown occurs. As long as you input decimal integers, scanf will accept up to eight of them in this example. As soon as anything but a decimal integer is input, the sequence is over. If you input

123456H

scanf assigns variable *i* the value of 1234 and *x* a value of 56. The printout from this program reads:

1234   56

The scanf function can be used to truncate numbers purposely. This is done in the program shown in Figure 4-14, which is designed to return the

Figure 4-14 Another scanf Program Limiting the Number of Digits that May Be Input.

```
main()
{
int i;
int x;
scanf("%3d %2d",&i,&x);
printf("\n\n");
printf("%d",i);
}
```

first three digits of a zip code for determination of mailing zones. The program is very similar to the previous one. However, the variable *i* is assigned a value of the first three digits, whereas variable *x* is assigned the value of the last two. The final printf line ignores the variable *x* altogether and simply prints the value of *i*, which has been extracted from the input at the keyboard. This is not a terribly good example of using scanf for extraction because the scanf line could have simply read:

$$scanf(``\%3d'',\&i);$$

Using this method, scanf shuts down as soon as the first three digits of the ZIP code are typed in and ignores the remaining two numbers, even if keys continue to be pressed. However, such a program is probably set up with a loop back to near the beginning, so the final two digits of the ZIP code are entered as the first two digits of the next ZIP code sequence. Also, while scanf is used to read input from the keyboard, there is another function in C named sscanf, which gets its input string from another string contained within a file. Such a file might contain the names of clients, along with their addresses and ZIP codes. Using sscanf, the ZIP code information—or even a select number of digits from the zip code—could be extracted. If you understand how to use scanf, you will also understand the sscanf operations for the most part.

Figure 4-15 shows a cleaned-up version of the ZIP code extraction program. Additional printf lines have been added to provide screen prompts, but the operation is basically the same. All five digits of the ZIP code are accepted at the input. The first three are passed on, while the last two are truncated from the screen display. Assuming an input of 22630, the printout will read:

THE ZONE DESIGNATION IS 226

This is only a small sampling of what scanf can do. These examples deal only with decimal integers. Later, we show how scanf can be used to make conversions, display characters, and so on. This is one of the most useful functions implemented in C, and this single function, along with its

```
main()
{
int i;
int x;
printf("INPUT ZIP CODE.\n\n");
scanf("%3d %2d",&i,&x);
printf("\n\n");
printf("THE ZONE DESIGNATION IS ");
printf("%d",i);
}
```

Figure 4-15 Modified Version of an Earlier Program Designed to Extract Zone Designations From a Complete ZIP Code.

conversion sequences and pointers, can effectively take the place of many, many lines in a program in BASIC that would accomplish the same machine function.

gets

The gets function in SuperSoft C is equivalent to the getline function in some other dialects of C. Gets is used to read an entire line from standard input (the keyboard). It is similar to the BASIC statement INPUT and, more specifically, INPUT A$.

Like getchar, the gets function suspends program execution until keyboard input has been read. Like the INPUT statement in BASIC, gets requires that the Enter key be pressed in order for program execution to continue.

The input received by the gets function is not displayed in the same manner demonstrated for displaying the input character obtained by the getchar function. To display string information of this type, a new function is brought into the picture. It is very similar to the printf function, but it is used to display keyboard input information in a manner more similar to the PRINT statement in BASIC.

This new function is puts; it is often used in conjunction with gets. An example is shown in Figure 4-16. Here, the variable *x* is identified as a character or character string (char x;). The information is obtained from keyboard input using the gets(x); function line. The printf function line is used simply to provide a double space between the input information, which is typed on the screen, and the reprinting of the same information, which is accomplished with the put(x); function line.

```
main()
{
char x;
gets(x);
printf("\n\n");
puts(x);
}
```

Figure 4-16   Program Demonstrating the gets and puts Functions of C Language.

These two functions are very aptly named because the gets function gets information from the keyboard and the puts function puts that same information on the screen. The puts function may also be used in a similar manner to printf by inserting quoted phrases within the parens that follow, as in:

puts("HOW ARE YOU."):

In SuperSoft C, puts is used exactly as fgets in other dialects of C, with the exception that the latter function is designed to pull information from a file, while puts pulls information from gets. This function is also quite similar to putchar.

When this program is run, you may type in any information at all and upon pressing Enter, the same information will be displayed two lines below the original input.

Floating Point Arithmetic

The previous chapter and most of this one deal mainly with the handling of numbers in C. All the mathematics involves integers. From a teaching standpoint, this is ideal at the beginning; however, it is also desirable to be able to perform other types of calculations that involve nonintegral numerical values. The SuperSoft C compiler used as a model in this book does not support these types of mathematical operations. However, future versions undoubtedly will. In any event, if you can write programs to perform arithmetic operations involving integers, you can do the same thing involving other types of numbers. The principle is exactly the same; only the designations are different.

Figure 4-17 shows a C program that will divide 13 by 6 and print the answer to one decimal place on the screen. Notice in the opening line of the program that the variable i is preceded by a float designator. This indicates that i will not be an integer, but rather a floating-point number, as opposed to int i;, which indicates that the variable i is an integer.

The next two variables, a and b, are indeed integers and are specified as such. The next program lines indicate the values of each variable. Notice that variable i is equal to a divided by b.

The printf function line is handled in nearly the same manner as when working with integers only. However, instead of a %d designation, a %f is used to specify a floating-point number. The machine is instructed to print a floating-point number at least two characters in width and with one digit after the decimal point. This means that the value of i will be given to an accuracy of one decimal place. If the printf function were changed to %2.2f, then i would be displayed with two characters following the decimal point.

You can see that floating-point mathematical operations are carried

```
main()
{
        float i;
        int a;
        int b;

        a=13;
        b=6;
        i=a/b;

        printf("%2.1f\n",i);
}
```

Figure 4-17 C Language Program Demonstrating Floating Point Arithmetic. (*Note:* This Program is not Compatible with the SuperSoft C Compiler.)

```
main()
{
    float i;

    i=13.0/6.0;

    printf("%2.1f\n",i);
}
```

Figure 4-18 Alternate Method of Writing the Program of Figure 4-17 in a Fewer Number of Lines.

out in a very similar manner to integer operations in C. It is necessary only to identify which variables are assigned what types of numbers. Figure 4-18 shows another way of writing the same program using fewer lines. Here, variables *a* and *b* have been eliminated and only the floating-point variable *i* is retained. Figure 4-19 shows an even simpler method of writing the program using no variables whatsoever. The printf function line is instructed to display on the screen the result of 13 divided by 6. You will notice that in both of the last two examples, 13.0/6.0 has been used rather than 13/6. While the latter may be conventional in other languages, it is not in C. A wrong answer will result if the decimal place designations are not included, as shown. This is due to the fact that integer division truncates any fractional parts, so without the decimal-point designations, the machine performs integer division rather than floating-point division. The answer to 13 divided by 6 in integer division is 2 because the fractional part is truncated. A decimal point in a constant indicates that it is a floating point, so 13.0 divided by 6.0 is 2.16666. Of course, the programs shown will display the answer as 2.1 because one decimal place is specified in the printf conversion specification.

Figure 4-19 Most Efficient Method of Writing Programs of Figures 4-17 and 4-18.

```
main()
{
    printf("%2.1f\n",13.0/6.0);
}
```

These programs will not run using version 1.1 of the SuperSoft C compiler because this version does not support floating-point arithmetic. As an experiment, you can input these programs, changing float i to int i; and %2.lf to %2d. You are set up again for integer math, so the fraction will always be truncated. Therefore, the output answer to 13/6 will be the same as the answer to 12/6, or 2.

Loops

In C programming language, loops are just as valuable as they are in other languages. In C, three types of loops are made available. Some loops have already been demonstrated, but others have not. We have already encountered the for loop, which is quite similar to the FOR-NEXT loop common to BASIC. Two other types of loops found in C involve the statements while and do. Therefore, there are three different methods that may be used for executing a set number of commands in a program. You will encounter the for and while loops much more often than the do loops, but all three have their uses.

```
main()
{
    int a;

    for(a=1;a<=15;++a)
        {
            printf("%d\n",a);
        }
```
Figure 4-20   A for Loop.   }

Figure 4-20 illustrates a for loop, which simply counts from 1 to 15 on the screen. The variable *a* is identified as an integer, and the minimum and maximum values, as well as its step factor, of the for statement line are assigned. Remember, in C, + + a means the same as A = A + 1 in BASIC. This brings about a loop count in steps of 1. The printf function line displays the changing values of *a*. Figure 4-21 shows the screen display when this program is run.

```
1
2
3
4
5
6
7
8
9
10
11
12
13
14
15
```
Figure 4-21 Program Run Using the Program of Figure 4-20.

Figure 4-22 shows an example of a while loop, which is used to accomplish the same thing as the for loop previously discussed. However, the printout of the program run shown in Figure 4-23 indicates that instead of counting from 1 to 15, the program is counted from 2 to 16. This occurs because this program was set up from the previous for loop demonstration program. The only real change that was made involved removing the for line and replacing it with while. The step count line was moved down into the executed portion of the loop. This new program activates the printf function whenever the value of *a* is less than or equal to 15. Before the printf function is activated, *a* is stepped by 1. Therefore, during the first cycle of the loop, *a*—which is already equal to 1—is stepped by 1 for a value of 2. It is then

```
main()
{

    int a;

    a=1;

    while(a<=15)
        {
        ++a;
        printf("%d\n",a);
        }
```

Figure 4-22   A while Loop.   }

printed on the screen. The loop goes through its second cycle, and the while line tests for a condition of *a* being equal to or less than 15. This value is still 2, so the loop cycles again, *a* is incremented by 1, and the value of 3 is printed.

```
2
3
4
5
6
7
8
9
10
11
12
13
14
15
16
```

Figure 4-23   Program Run of while Loop Program.

   While this portion of the printout is easy to understand, people often ask why the printout counts to 16 when the loop instructions are to terminate when the value of *a* is more than 15. This is a reasonable query and, indeed, the loop does terminate when *a* is equal to 16. However, you must remember that the printf function line will always display a value of *a* which is 1 higher than the actual value detected by the loop. When *a* is 15, the loop goes through another cycle. However, the value of 15 is incremented by 1 (+ + a) before it is printed. Therefore, the final value printed on the screen is 16. Since *a* is now equal to 16, the loop shuts down and the program is effectively terminated. In order to get a matching count when compared to that of the for loop previously discussed, it is necessary only to change the value of *a* to 0 instead of 1 and change the top value in the while statement line to 14. An easier way, however, is to simply switch the printf function line and the + + a line, leaving everything else as shown in Figure 4-22. In this case, the screen write occurs before the value of *a* is incremented. Either of these modifications will give you a count of 1 to 15.

   Figure 4-24 demonstrates a do loop, which is also known as a do-while loop. The differences between a do-while loop and a while loop are quite

```
main()
{
        int a;
        a=0;
        do
                {
                ++a;
                printf("%d\n",a);
                }
        while(a<=15);
```

Figure 4-24   A do-while Loop.   }

subtle. In this example, I have tried to set up a program that will count from 1 to 15. However, Figure 4-25 shows that the loop actually counts from 1 to 16. This again is due to the fact that the step line (+ + a) is located previous to the printf function line. You will notice, however, that the value of a is 0 at the start. If the maximum value of the while statement line were changed to

```
1
2
3
4
5
6
7
8
9
10
11
12
13
14
15
```

Figure 4-25   A do-while Program Run.   16

14, the count would be proper. Figure 4-26 shows another method of obtaining a 1 to 15 count, which simply involves switching the printf and incrementing lines and changing the starting value of a to 1. In both examples, the lines within the braces following the do statement are executed in light of a specific situation. In this case, the while statement indicates the nature of that condition. The do-while loop operates in an opposite manner to a FOR-NEXT loop in BASIC. Using a FOR-NEXT loop as an example, the minimum, maximum, and step values of the loop are determined by the opening

```
main()
{
        int a;
        a=1;
        do
                {
                printf("%d\n",a);
                ++a;
                }
        while(a<=15);
```

Figure 4-26   Alternate do-while Program.   }

statement (FOR). The NEXT statement simply acts as a return as long as a specified condition is true. The opposite occurs in a do-while loop. It is the ending statement (while) that determines the number of loop cycles.

All three loops may be used interchangeably in many programming applications, but as you delve deeper into C, you will find that each has its own special abilities and one will probably stand out above the rest given any particular complex loop assignment.

Summary

This chapter delves into a number of useful functions and statements common to C programming language. These are the functions and statements that you will use in almost every programming assignment. Their uses are explained and depicted in actual programs, which should run on your machine. By no means has each and every use of these functions and statements been discussed. The examples shown in this chapter are to serve as a basic guide to get you started. I highly recommend that you input and run each program presented here and then make changes in order to get each to perform slightly different functions. Only through this trial-and-error experimentation can you become fully knowledgeable about the capabilities each has to offer.

5 **HANDLING**
CHARACTER STRINGS

The previous chapters deal mainly with numerical and arithmetical operations in C programming language, but this one concentrates on the use of alphabetical characters, words, and sentences. In many instances, only a few programming changes are necessary to convert from numerical values to alphabetic values. Also, C is rich in functions that are designed specifically for converting, comparing, and testing alphabetic and/or numeric strings. Your basic start in programming in C is not complete until you can handle alphabetic strings as easily as numeric strings. This chapter goes a long way toward introducing you to the functions and statements used to handle the inputting of words and phrases.

When dealing with variables in C programming language, you must specify the variable type before you perform any operations using them. The variable type with which we are most familiar at this juncture is int. When used preceding a variable, int indicates that the variable will be a numeric value, and more specifically, an integer. When handling characters of an alphabetic nature, the char type-specifier is used. This indicates that the variable will consist of characters, as opposed to integers or floating-point numbers, which are identified by type-specifiers int and float.

Figure 5-1 shows a program that was discussed previously. Here, the variable x is identified as an integer. Getchar is used to accept a single character from the keyboard. Since x is an integer, the character received from the keyboard is the ASCII equivalent of the keyboard character. If you input a capital X, the ASCII equivalent is 88 and, therefore, the output from this program will be a number 88 on the display screen.

```
main()
{
    int x;

    x=getchar();

    printf("\n\n");
    printf("%d\n",x);
}
```

Figure 5-1 Using a getchar to Return an Integer.

Figure 5-2 shows the same basic program, only in this case, i is the variable. It is specified as a character variable using the char type-specifier. Again, getchar is used to accept a character from the keyboard. As in the previous example, the printf function line is simply used to insert a double space between the input line and the screen write line. In this case, the screen write is accomplished with the putchar function. This writes the character i

```
main()
{
char i;
i=getchar();
printf("\n\n");
putchar(i);
}
```

Figure 5-2 Using a getchar to Return a Character.

to the standard output, which, in this case, is the screen. When you input any letter, the same letter will appear two lines below. Getchar accepts the character and putchar displays it on the screen.

Now, suppose you want to display the character and its ASCII number as well. Recall that in a previous program, the ASCII character could be displayed by using the printf function in conjunction with the integer variable. In this case, however, the variable is a char type, so a conversion must be made. The program shown in Figure 5-3 accomplishes this. Here, there are two variable assignments. The first one is a character type (*x*), while the second is an integer (*i*). The character is accepted from the keyboard using getchar. Now, when getchar is used, the character that is input is automatically terminated with a null character represented by 0. In other words, when using getchar, typing in the capital letter *H* appears as H/0. This is very similar to the slash-n escape sequence used with printf.

```
main()
{
        char x;
        int i;

        x=getchar();

        i=x-'0';

        printf("\n\n");
        printf("%d\n",i);
        putchar(x);
}
```

Figure 5-3   This Program Uses getchar to Return Both a Character and an Integer Value.

The next line in the program converts the character *x* to an integer. Remember, variable *x* has been assigned the value of the capital letter *H*. However, to make a truly accurate conversion, it is necessary to remove the null escape sequence from the end of the variable. This is accomplished by allowing *i* to be equal to variable *x* − '0';. The next line adds a double space, and the next printf line then displays the integer value of the keyboard character on the screen. In this case, the value will be 72, since this is the ASCII value of the capital letter *H*. Then, putchar is used to place the character assigned to the variable *x* on the screen. This, of course, is the capital letter *H*. When this program is run and an *H* is typed in on the keyboard, the screen will display the number 72 and below it the capital letter *H*.

An earlier chapter states that puts often accompanies gets, or putchar often accompanies getchar, in displaying a string on the screen. While this is common practice, printf may also be used. We demonstrate this using the gets function. Figure 5-4 shows a simple program that accepts a string character value from the keyboard and then reprints it two lines below the input line. Here, the variable *i* is specified as a character. Gets accepts the keyboard input. When Enter is pressed, the printf function adds the double

```
main()
{
char i;
gets(i);
printf("\n\n");
puts(i);
}
```

Figure 5-4 Program That Accepts String Character Value From the Keyboard and Reprints it Two Lines Below.

space and the puts function is used to display the original input string at the new position on the screen. If you type in hello, this string of characters will be repeated two lines below the input line.

However, the same thing may be accomplished in a different manner using printf, as Figure 5-5 demonstrates. The program is identical to the previous one, with the exception of the last line. Here, printf has been used to replace puts. Previous uses of printf have included conversion specifications of %d and %f. The first denotes an integer, while the second indicates a floating-point number. However, this printf function line uses %s. This new conversion specification indicates that the value of *i* to be displayed is a string. Again, if you input hello, the same word will appear two lines below the original input line. You can see that extra programming is required to accomplish the same function in this manner. It's far easier to program puts(i); than to type in the entire printf line. Either option is available to you, however.

```
main()
{
char i;
gets(i);
printf("\n\n");
printf("%s\n\n",i);
}
```

Figure 5-5 Different Method of Obtaining the Same Results of the Program in Figure 5-4.

String Processing Functions

C programming language has a number of functions that have been designed specifically for comparing character strings and even merging them. These can serve a number of useful functions and are instrumental as programming aids in any program that makes use of character strings. Each of these functions has a rough equivalent in BASIC, but using the latter language, several program lines would be necessary, whereas in C, a single function line alone will usually suffice. These very powerful functions point to the reason for the increased use of C by software companies who write word-processing programs for many different types of machines. Remember, once the C program is compiled, it is in executable form and may be run on any machine whose microprocessor is the target microprocessor of the compiler.

strcat

The strcat function is used to add strings. It is followed by two variable
designators, which indicate the order in which the string combination is to be
handled. The program shown in Figure 5-6 demonstrates the use of this function quite simply. Here, variables *a* and *b* are specified as characters. The
printf function line is used to prompt the operator about his or her respon-

```
{
char a,b;
printf("ENTER ANY WORD\n");
gets(a);
printf("ENTER ANOTHER WORD\n");
gets(b);
strcat(a,b);
puts(a);
}
```

Figure 5-6   Using the strcat Function.

sibility. The first prompt tells the operator to enter any word. The next line
contains the gets function, which assigns the keyboard input to the char
variable *a*. As soon as this has been accomplished, another prompt appears,
telling the operator to enter yet another word. It is at this point that the strcat
function enters the program. This line tells the machine to add string *b* to the
end of string *a*. String *a* now contains its original input plus the contents of
string *b*. The puts function is used to display the newly reconstructed string *a*
on the screen. Figure 5-7 shows a sample program run.

```
ENTER ANY WORD
hello
ENTER ANOTHER WORD
GOODBYE
helloGOODBYE
```

Figure 5-7   strcat Program Run.

You first see the prompt in capital letters and below it, the keyboard input hello in lowercase letters. As soon as Enter is pressed, another prompt
appears, and this time, the input string is the word GOODBYE. When Enter
is pressed again, the strcat function is used to combine the two, and the result
is helloGOODBYE.

Figure 5-8 shows a more practical example of how this program might
be used. Upon the first prompt, the phrase THE CORRECT TIME IS is
entered. When the second prompt appears, the operator inputs ONE A.M.
When the strings are combined, the result is quite obvious.

```
ENTER ANY WORD
THE CORRECT TIME IS
ENTER ANOTHER WORD
ONE A.M.
THE CORRECT TIME IS ONE A.M.
```

Figure 5-8   A More-Practical Use of the
Program in Figure 5-6.

While this program has linked the *b* string to the end of *a,* the exact opposite could have been done just as easily. All that is necessary to effect this is a change in the strcat function line to:

strcat(b,a);

The next line is changed to:

puts(b);

This reverses the order of the combined printout.

In actual use, strcat might be seen many times and used to link a whole glossary of words together in an intelligible sentence. Instead of two variables, 200 or more might be used to perform a highly complex word-processing operation.

strlen

Another valuable function used to handle strings in C programming language is strlen, which is easily compared with the LEN function in BASIC. In this latter language, LEN is used effectively to count the number of characters in any string, and this is almost exactly how strlen is used in C. The strlen function returns the number of characters in the string specified.

Figure 5-9 demonstrates this. Here, *i* is assigned an integer value, while *x* is a character value. The string value hello is assigned to *x,* while *i* is equal to the strlen value of the *x* variable. The printf function line is used to display the value of *x,* which, in this case, is 5. When used with gets and/or getchar, the null terminating values associated with these keyboard input functions are not counted by strlen. Any other character is; of course, this includes spaces. The string value of how are you is 11 because there are 9 characters and 2 spaces.

Figure 5-10 shows a slightly more-complex program, which uses strlen

```
main()
{

int i;
char x;

x="hello"

i=strlen(x);

printf("%d\n",i);

}
```

Figure 5-9 Program That Demonstrates the strlen Function.

```
main()
{   '
int i;
int h;
char a,b;
printf("ENTER ANY WORD OR NUMBER\n");
gets(a);
h=strlen(a);
printf("ENTER ANOTHER WORD OR NUMBER\n");
gets(b);
i=strlen(b);
if(i==h)
puts("THE TWO STRINGS ARE IDENTICAL IN CHARACTER LENGTH\n");
else
puts("THE TWO STRINGS ARE NOT EQUAL IN CHARACTER LENGTH\n");
}
```

Figure 5-10   A More-Complex Program That Uses strlen to Compare Two Strings.

to compare two strings in order to tell whether or not they contain identical characters links. Actually, strlen is used twice because the purpose of this program is to compare two strings. The string values are assigned to integer variables *i* and *h*. The string information from the keyboard is assigned to the char variables *a* and *b,* respectively.

The printf function lines are used to display screen prompts. The first string is accepted by the gets(a) function line. The number of characters in this line is returned by strlen(a); in the next line and is assigned to the integer variable *h*. The next three lines repeat the previous three, but for the second string, which is assigned to the variable *b*. The strlen value of this line is assigned to the integer variable *i*.

At this point, an if statement compares the two strings. If the two are equal, the puts function immediately below the if statements is activated and the screen prompt it contains is displayed. Printf could just as easily have been used here instead of puts. In this mode, the two are interchangeable. However, puts cannot be used with conversion specifiers discussed elsewhere. If the values of *i* and *h* are not identical, the last puts function line is activated, indicating that the character links are not the same. Figure 5-11 shows an example of a typical program run. Here, the first word input is

```
ENTER ANY WORD OR NUMBER
HELLO
ENTER ANOTHER WORD OR NUMBER
HELLOS
THE TWO STRINGS ARE NOT EQUAL IN CHARACTER LENGTH
```

Figure 5-11   Sample Run Using the Program of Figure 5-10.

HELLO. The second word input is HELLOS. The first word contains five letters, while the second contains six. Therefore the nonidentical prompt is activated, as shown. Figure 5-12 shows another program run. Here, each of the input strings contains five characters, so the identical prompt appears

```
ENTER ANY WORD OR NUMBER
HELLO
ENTER ANOTHER WORD OR NUMBER
12345
THE TWO STRINGS ARE IDENTICAL IN CHARACTER LENGTH
```

Figure 5-12 Another Program Run Demonstrating the Use of strlen.

once the two strings have been rated. Notice in this second example that a numerical string value has been used for the second input. This is perfectly acceptable, but remember that this is a string value and cannot be treated as an integer value, which might involve certain mathematical operations. As demonstrated previously, however, a character string value can be converted to an integer value.

strcmp

The strcmp function (string compare) compares one string with another. Unlike strlen, which compares character number content of two strings, strcomp compares two strings on a character-by-character basis. For two strings to be identical, each string must contain the same number of characters, and each character must be identical on a position-by-position basis. Figure 5-13 shows a program that uses strcmp to compare two strings. This is handled in much the same manner as the previous programs. Once the

```
main()
{

char a,b;
printf("ENTER ANY WORD OR NUMBER\n");
gets(a);
printf("ENTER ANOTHER WORD OR NUMBER\n");
gets(b);
if(!strcmp(a,b))
puts("THE TWO STRINGS ARE IDENTICAL\n");
else
puts("THE TWO STRINGS ARE NOT EQUAL\n");

}
```

Figure 5-13 Program That Uses strcmp to Compare Two Strings.

two strings have been gathered from the keyboard and assigned to variables *a* and *b,* respectively, the if statement does the rest of the work. This is a slightly abbreviated form of programming. The exclamation mark at the beginning of the portion of this line in parentheses indicates equal. What this line says is to compare string *a* with string *b,* and if they are equal, then execute the puts function line immediately following. The else statement in-

```
ENTER ANY WORD OR NUMBER
hello
ENTER ANOTHER WORD OR NUMBER
goodbye
THE TWO STRINGS ARE NOT EQUAL
```

Figure 5-14 Typical Run of the Program in Figure 5-13.

dicates the function to be executed in the event the two are not equal. Figure 5-14 shows a program run in which the two strings are not equal, while Figure 5-15 shows another program run in which equal string values have been input.

```
ENTER ANY WORD OR NUMBER
hello
ENTER ANOTHER WORD OR NUMBER
hello
THE TWO STRINGS ARE IDENTICAL
```

Figure 5-15 Program Run in Which Equal String Values Have Been Input.

To demonstrate a more practical use of the strcmp function, consider the program in Figure 5-16. This is a very simple computer quiz. It uses several of the functions discussed in this and previous chapters. The identifier QRP: indicates a branch to point. Variables *a* and *b* are specified as character variables, while *i* is an integer. The string value assigned to *a* is the correct answer to the question that will be asked in the following printf line.

```
main()
{
QRP:
int i;
char a,b;
a="WASHINGTON";        a = "Washington;
printf("Who was the first president of the United States?\n");
gets(b);
if(!strcmp(a,b))
{
printf("That is a correct answer!!\n"); exit(i);
}
printf("That answer is wrong! Press any key to try again.\n");
getchar();
goto QRP;
}
```

Figure 5-16 Computer Quiz Program Using strcmp.

The gets function is used to retrieve the user's answer from the keyboard. At this point, the strcmp function compares string *a* (the correct answer) with string *b* (the keyboard input). If the two are correct, the correct answer prompt is displayed. Notice that this line contains two functions. They are separated by semicolons, as required in C. If the answer is correct, the exit function is used to terminate the program. On the other hand, if string *a* and string *b* do not compare, the wrong answer prompt appears, and getchar is used to halt program execution. When any character is typed in via the

keyboard, execution continues and the goto statement in the next line
branches to the beginning of the program, where the question is asked again.
The program will continue to run until the correct answer is input or until the
program is manually halted. The answer must be input exactly as it appears
in the program; that is, the first letter must be a capital *W* and the rest lowercase letters. An input of all capital letters will be registered as a wrong
answer. Figure 5-17 shows a typical program run.

```
Who was the first president of the United States?
Lincoln
That answer is wrong! Press any key to try again.

Who was the first president of the United States?
Washington
That is a correct answer!!
```

Figure 5-17   Typical Program Run.

strcpy

The strcpy function in C programming language simply copies one string
into another. It can convert a string, or it can reassign a string value. Figure
5-18 shows a typical use of strcpy. Here, the user is prompted to input one
string and then another. The strcpy function is used to write the contents of
string *b* into string *a*. If the number of characters in string *b* is equivalent to
the number in string *a*, then string *b* will simply replace *a*. If there are fewer
characters in string *b* than in string *a,* then all string *b* will be written over the
first characters in string *a,* with the remaining characters in string *a* appearing at the end.

For example, if you input hello for the first string and yellow for the
second string, the output from this program is the word yellow. However, if
yellow is input for the first string and hello for the second, the output is
hellow. The first five characters of the second string (hello) are written over
the first five characters of the first string.

```
main()
{
char a,b;
printf("ENTER ANY WORD OR NUMBER\n");
gets(a);
printf("ENTER ANOTHER WORD OR NUMBER\n");
gets(b);
strcpy(a,b);
puts(a);
}
```

Figure 5-18   Program That Demonstrates the strcpy Function.

Upper/Lower Case Functions

Several functions are available (often used as matched sets) in C programming language to detect and/or convert uppercase and lowercase characters. The detection functions include isupper and islower. The islower function detects a lowercase character. These two functions apply only to the character keys themselves, not to the number keys. The conversion functions are toupper and tolower, which are used to convert from one case to another.

The program shown in Figure 5-19 fully demonstrates the use of all four of these functions. Here, the variable x is identified as a char type and QRP: is used as a return identifier (to be matched with a subsequent goto statement). A single character is accepted from the keyboard using the getchar function. The next series of lines uses the four detection/conversion functions previously discussed. Each one of these functions is tied into the character variable x. The first if statement line tests for a condition of variable x being equal to an uppercase keyboard character. If variable x is an uppercase character, the following putchar function is executed. Here, the tolower function comes into play. This line tells the machine to write the lowercase version of the uppercase character assigned to variable x. If you input an uppercase W, a lowercase w will be printed immediately to its right.

If the input character is lowercase, the next two program lines take over. Here, islower is coupled with an if statement. This line tells the computer that if the character assigned to x is lowercase, the next line is to be executed. In this line, a putchar function is coupled with toupper to display on the screen the uppercase equivalent of the lowercase character assigned to x. The following printf statement inserts a line space and carriage return and the goto statement then branches to near the beginning of the program. The

```
main()
{

    char x;

QRP:

    x=getchar();

    if(isupper(x))
    {
     putchar(tolower(x));
    }
    if(islower(x))
    {
     putchar(toupper(x));
    }

    printf("\n");

    goto QRP;

}
```

Figure 5-19 Program That Demonstrates the Uppercase/Lowercase Functions.

program run is on a continuous loop, and you may input as many keyboard characters as you desire before manually halting the program. Figure 5-20 shows a sample program run. Note that if the first character is lowercase, the one to its right is uppercase. The reverse is true when the first character is upper case.

```
j J
S s
X x
C c
V v
B b
N n
M m
p P
1 L
k K
o O
i I
u U
y Y
```

Figure 5-20 Typical Run of the Program in Figure 5-19.

Figure 5-21 shows another run of this program, into which a few numbers have been inserted. The numbers are displayed on the screen (due to the getchar function). To avoid an erroneous input, other functions are available in C programming language. These are more often referred to as

```
j J
r R
D d
2 2
f F
8 8
X x
c C
9 9
" "
h H
M m
```

Figure 5-21 Program Run in Which Numbers and Punctuation Marks Have Been Intermingled With Characters.

macros and include isupper, islower, tolower, toupper, and two new ones, isdigit and isalpha. The first one determines whether or not an input character is a digit. The second one tests for a character. The program in Figure 5-22 shows a use of isdigit inserted into the previous program to prevent an erroneous keyboard input from being passed on to the major processing portions of the program. The program is very much like the previous one, with the exception of the if statement line containing the isdigit macro. This line and the following goto statement are used to branch back to the beginning of the program when a digit is input via the keyboard, since this program is designed to process characters only. The if statement line simply tells the machine that if the variable x contains a digit rather than a character, then goto QRP:. If the variable x is not a digit, then the program

```
main()
{

    char x;

QRP:

    x=getchar();
    if(isdigit(x))
    {
    goto QRP;
    }

    if(isupper(x))
    {
     putchar(tolower(x));
    }
    if(islower(x))
    {
     putchar(toupper(x));
    }
    printf("\n");
    goto QRP;
}
```

Figure 5-22   Use of the isdigit Function.

processes the keyboard information as before. Figure 5-23 shows a typical program run. You can see that three digits have been inserted, and while these are displayed on the screen, no conversion takes place.

The isalpha macro is used in the same manner as isdigit, but it tests for an alphabetical character having been input from the keyboard. The program shown in Figure 5-24 demonstrates isalpha when used in a program

```
qQ
wW
eE
rR
tT
yY
6
Kk
8
Mm
1
Hh
aA
sS
dD
fF
gG
gG
bB
nN
mM
zZ
xX
cC
```

Figure 5-23   Program Run of isdigit Demonstration Program.

```
main()
{

    char x;

QRP:

    x=getchar();

    if(isalpha(x))
    {
     goto QRP;
    }

    int y;

    y=x-'01';

    printf("%d\n", y);

}
```

Figure 5-24 Program That Demonstrates
the isalpha Function.

that is designed to accept only integer information. Here, char x is to be a
numerical digit from the keyboard. Letters are not acceptable. Therefore,
isalpha is used to detect an alphabetic character and branch back to the getchar function when this type of erroneous input is read.

scanf

The scanf function is discussed earlier in the text, but it bears further study in
this chapter because it is an extremely valuable tool in C language. It may be
used to collect many different types of information and is probably the best
comparison with the INPUT statement in BASIC. Scanf can be used in conjunction with printf to reformat file and input information. In some ways, it
can be used to take the place (in conjunction with printf) of strcat.

Figure 5-25 shows a program which combines scanf and printf to

```
main()
{

    char x[50];
    char y[50];
    char z[50];

    scanf("%5s %3s %3s",&x,&y,&z);

    printf("\n\n");
    printf("%3s %5s %3s\n",y,x,z);
    printf("%3s %3s %5s\n",z,y,x);
    printf("%3s %3s %5s\n",y,z,x);
    printf("%s %s %s\n",x,y,z);
    printf("%7s %8s %14s",x,y,z);

}
```

Figure 5-25 Program That Combines
scanf and printf to Arrive at a Prearranged Screen Display Format.

display either characters or digits in a prearranged format on the screen. Here, variables *x, y,* and *z* are specified as characters (char), and each is assigned a maximum bit length by the numbers appearing in brackets following each variable name. In this example, the bit length is unimportant as long as it is at least equal to the number of characters read by the scanf function. The scanf function line determines the number of characters that it will read. The %s conversion specification indicates that it will read string characters rather than integer values.

The scanf line will assign the first five characters input via the keyboard to the variable *x*. The next three are assigned to the variable *y*, while the following three are assigned to *z*. Notice that the arguments in the scanf line are pointers, indicated by the ampersand (&) immediately preceding them.

The first printf line is used to insert a double space between the input that has been typed on the screen and the printf lines that follow. Screen formatting of information is handled in the next five lines, all of which use printf functions. Note that the first three printf lines in this series have rearranged the placement of variables *x, y,* and *z*. Recall that the assignments were made in alphabetical order, but these lines mix up this order. The fourth line once again arranges information in alphabetical order, and you will notice that no character-width designators are used in the conversion specifications (%s instead of %3s, for example). The last printf line uses character-width designators that are larger than those specified in the scanf line. Figure 5-26 shows a sample program run. The phrase *thereyouare* was input, and the next five lines indicate the reformatting of this initial value.

```
                      thereyouare

                      you there are
                      are you there
                      you are there
                      there you are
                        there      you              are
```

Figure 5-26   Typical Run of the Program in Figure 5-25.

The fourth line reprints the original information, with the exception that spaces are included between each word. These spaces were actually determined by the variable assignments in the scanf line. The first three lines also contain spaces, but since the character-width numerical specifications in the conversion specification figures were no larger than those in the scanf conversion specifications, such designators are superfluous. The printf line (second from the bottom), which contains no numerical designators, serves well. However, the last line shows what happens when character-width designators are of higher values than those specified in scanf. This is true onscreen formatting, which allows you to place words at different points on the screen and rearrange word placement when compared with the initial input.

Figure 5-27 shows another run of this program with a digit input via the keyboard.

The first function discussed in this exploration of C language was printf. At first glance, it seemed to be a fairly mundane function, but with conversion specifications and proper coupling to such functions as scanf, getchar, or gets, it becomes an extremely powerful tool.

```
12345678999

678 12345 999
999 678 12345
678 999 12345
12345 678 999
 12345      678              999
```

Figure 5-27 Alternate Program Run Illustrating the Result of a Digit Input.

sleep

SuperSoft C includes some functions that have been added to the original version of the C programming language developed by Bell Laboratories. One of these is the sleep function, which is used very much like a time-delay loop consisting of FOR-NEXT statements in BASIC. This function is aptly named, because it is designed to suspend program execution for a certain period of time, putting the machine in the sleep mode. The actual sleep period is determined by the value coupled with the sleep function. The program shown in Figure 5-28 demonstrates the use of the sleep function. When the program is run, a prompt line indicates that this is a demonstration of the sleep function. The function itself is used in the next line and is coupled with the number 200. The actual sleep period will depend on the internal clock frequency of your microcomputer, but, generally speaking, the number is in tenths of seconds. In this example, the execution halt will be for approximately 200 tenths of a second, or 20 seconds. Adjustments can be made to determine nearly exact sleep times through trial-and-error experimentation with this function on your machine.

```
main()
{
    printf("SLEEP(n) function demo.\n\n");

    sleep(200);

    printf("End demo.\n\n");
}
```

Figure 5-28 Program Demonstrating the sleep Function.

```
main()
{

    int n;

    n=200;

    printf("The purpose of this program is to demonstrate\n\n");
    printf("the use of the SLEEP(n) function in C Programming\n\n");
    printf("Language. This function suspends execution for\n\n");
    printf("the approximate equivalent of n-tenths of a\n\n");
    printf("second on microcomputers operating at a\n\n");
    printf("clock frequency of about 4 megahertz. \n\n");
    printf("Those machines which operate at higher\n\n");
    printf("or lower internal clock frequencies will\n\n");
    printf("exhibit shorter and longer 'sleep' times.\n\n");
    printf("The SLEEP() function is useful in creat-\n\n");
    printf("ing time delays during a program run,\n\n");
    printf("especially those involving long screen displays.\n\n");

    sleep(n);

    printf("\n\n\n\n\n\n\n\n\n\n\n\n\n\n\n\n");

    printf("In this example, SLEEP(n) was used to allow\n\n");
    printf("an adequate amount of time for the screen\n\n");
    printf("information to be read before scrolling on\n\n");
    printf("to the next screen page.\n\n");
}
```

Figure 5–29   A Program That Uses the sleep Function to Allow for the Convenient Display of a Large Amount of Information on the Screen.

When the sleep function is encountered, execution halts for the specified period of time. The sleep function is useful when it is necessary to display more than a full screen of information at any one time. As you know, when the screen is completely filled, additional lines produce scrolling and the top lines are lost. In BASIC, a FOR-NEXT loop is often used to halt temporarily the display of information on the screen until the operator has had time to read what is displayed. When the loop times out, execution of the PRINT lines continues, since the previous information that is now scrolling off the screen is no longer needed. The sleep function in C does not actually suspend execution, but it causes the machine to enter a similar loop, which times out after the specified number of one-tenth second units has elapsed. The program shown in Figure 5-29 demonstrates the usefulness of the sleep function in displaying text information that fills more than an entire screen. Figure 5-30 shows the result of the program run. This information spans the equivalent of about $1\frac{1}{2}$ screens. The top portion fills the entire screen. All screen writing halts for 20 seconds or so upon encountering the sleep function. After this period of time, the remaining information is displayed.

```
B>samp1
MSDOS Run time V1.2.29  Copyright 1983 SuperSoft
The purpose of this program is to demonstrate

the use of the SLEEP(n) function in C Programming

Language. This function suspends execution for

the approximate equivalent of n-tenths of a

second on microcomputers operating at a

clock frequency of about 4 megahertz.

Those machines which operate at higher

or lower internal clock frequencies will

exhibit shorter and longer 'sleep' times.

The SLEEP() function is useful in creat-

ing time delays during a program run,

especially those involving long screen displays.
```

```
In this example, SLEEP(n) was used to allow

an adequate amount of time for the screen

information to be read before scrolling on

to the next screen page.
```

Figure 5-30   Results of the Program in Figure 5-29 During Execution.

 PROGRAMS IN C LANGUAGE

This chapter includes several complete programs written in C language. These programs are simple, but are designed to use many of the functions and statements which have already been discussed. The scope of this book does not include the full exploration of every function, statement, and operation available in C. Only those functions basic to the use of the language have been discussed in any great detail. It is not possible to learn a new language (effectively) by simply hearing an explanation of each function and statement. It is necessary to concentrate on a few functions and statements, find out specifically how they are used in programs, and then experiment on your own—preferably backed up by a C reference source, which will allow for further exploration of other functions that may work in a similar manner to those with which you are already familiar. For example, previous chapters in this book deal with printf, scanf, gets, and puts, among others. Other functions that operate in a similar manner to these include fprintf, fscanf, fgets, and fputs. Each of these functions is equivalent or almost equivalent to its base function (the one without the preceding *f*), except that instead of writing information to the screen or pulling it from the keyboard, these activities take place in surrounding files. For example, fprintf will write information to a specified file rather than the screen. To deal with printf and then fprintf can be quite confusing before proper knowledge has been obtained regarding getchar, scanf, and other functions. However, once a moderate complement of input/output and display functions has been mastered regarding the keyboard and the display screen (standard input and output), it takes only a short while to gain a full understanding of the file-handling equivalents of these functions.

For this reason, the majority of information contained in this text as far as a discussion of functions and statements is concerned deal with the standard input and output. The matters of file establishment and handling, as well as other areas of this multifaceted language, are left for another study arena.

The programs presented in this chapter use most of the functions and statements already discussed and introduce a few new ones. The types of programs were chosen somewhat at random, but also because they accomplish many of the same things some of the first full programs in BASIC did for you during the early phases of your computer training. As a matter of fact, some of the programs in this chapter are simply conversions, having been written directly from programs in BASIC. Others, however, demonstrate the ease of programming that C offers anyone with just a small amount of knowledge of this new language.

Perhaps the programs contained in this chapter will be more valuable to you than some of the others that have already been discussed. While most of the previous programs can and should be compiled and run as shown, many might be considered subroutines, and all fall into the category of programming blocks. The programs presented and discussed in this chapter, likewise, may be compiled and run as shown. However, they represent entire programming concepts rather than individual portions of a more complex program setup. Even so, you may want to make modifications, improvements, and additions. This type of experimentation can add greatly to your C programming education. However, I do recommend that you input the programs exactly as shown, compile them, and then try a test run *before* attempting any serious modifications. In this manner, you will be certain that you are starting with a working program, one that does not contain any typographical errors that might affect the initial run. As soon as you see what the program does or can do, then you are free to make modifications and note the results of these changes during the next compilation and run sequence.

An earlier chapter explains how the programs presented here were compiled and run using an IBM Personal Computer with MS-DOS. The system outlined for compiling and testing these programs was suggested to offer the speediest time possible between actually writing the program (using EDLIN) and compiling, assembling, and linking it, in order to end up with a version that can be executed immediately. This method, however, cannot be recommended for general programming applications. The fault lies mainly with the fact that the method I have suggested links all the library files (CRUNT2, FORMATIO, STDIO, ALLOC, FUNC, etc.) with each C program. Each of these files contains different functions, and in some cases, only a single function has been called in a C program. In such cases, it is necessary to link only the library file containing that function. The rest are not needed. Normally, #INCLUDE language extensions are used at the beginning of the C program (while it is being written using the line editor). These extensions include the C language version of the library file in the program itself. Both are compiled as one executable program. For example, if you write a C program that contains only a single function, such as printf, it may be necessary to use only the FORMATIO standard library file, because this function is contained therein. Using the system outlined in an earlier chapter, the program would be written and FORMATIO, along with all the other standard library files, would then be linked to it. This would mean that all other files, with the exception of FORMATIO, would simply go along for the ride and use up valuable memory space. As a matter of fact, about the smallest memory usage required to compile a simple program used to print your name would be about 16,000 bytes. The C program itself takes up only 20 bytes or so. The rest is required to contain the linked library files. This is very poor programming from an efficiency standpoint. From a tutorial view, it is very efficient from your standpoint because it is not necessary to search through a C program and the standard library files in an attempt to discover which files must be included with the program in order to achieve a successful run. In other words, by including *all* the standard library files, you can be assured that if a program fails to run, it is probably due to some programming error and not a failure to include the needed functions.

The SuperSoft C compiler is accompanied by good documentation, and it takes only a short while to memorize the standard library files and, generally, the functions each contains. At this point, you may wish to streamline your programming (from a memory standpoint) and use the # INCLUDE preprocessor directive to incorporate the entire file containing the desire function or functions into your program. For example:

```
# INCLUDE FORMATIO.C
main ( )
{
printf("hello \ n");
}
```

is a program that will print hello on the screen and consume far less storage space because the preprocessor directive is used. During the linking stage, it is necessary to link only the minimum number of modules required with your C package. With my SuperSoft package, this is PREF + CPROGRAM + POST. It is not necessary to link FORMATIO, since that file is already a part of CPROGRAM.

You will notice that the preprocessor directive names FORMATIO.C rather than FORMATIO.OBJ. If you have the MS-DOS version of the SuperSoft C compiler, you will find both files available on the diskette. The files that contain the .C extension are simply C language programs that have not been compiled. On the other hand, FORMATIO.OBJ is the same C program that has been compiled and assembled and is ready to be used by the link program.

When you use the # INCLUDE preprocessor directive, the compiler sees this as part of your C language program and treats both as one complex program. In this case, the library file is far more complex than the sample C program. Nevertheless, it must be included in order for this simple program to run.

You should see immediately that this is a far more efficient way of writing and compiling programs, but only from a storage standpoint. The main disadvantage of using the # INCLUDE preprocessor directive lies in speed of compilation. If you must # INCLUDE two or three library files, it may be 20 minutes or more before even a small C program is completely compiled, assembled, and linked into an executable program. Of course, once this is done, it should not have to be done again, but this assumes that you are writing a program to be used over and over again rather than one that will be modified many times and used as a study of C language.

Let's assume that it takes 10 minutes to convert a program to executable form. When this program is run, an imperfection may surface, and it may be necessary to make a slight change in one of your program lines. It then takes another 10 minutes to compile the program again. If you're going to make many different changes based upon several program runs, you could easily be hours in developing a finished product. From an experimentation standpoint, this method is not very practical, in my opinion. If you have plenty of memory space (double-density diskette storage or hard disk, for example), program size may not be of extreme importance. In most of my early experimentation, I simply linked the precompiled and assembled standard library object modules to the program, as suggested earlier. I had enough space on diskette to safely hold one executable program. The rest of the space on the 320K diskettes was consumed by the compiler itself, the assembler, and the linker. However, when I arrived at an executable program that tested satisfactorily, I would simply save the uncompiled C program from which it was made, erase the executable version, and then write another program. It was a simple matter to recompile the first program if it was needed again. This took only a few minutes.

A good compromise here is to remove the linking procedure from any batch files and do this manually at the keyboard input. This is the best trade-off, as it then gives you the capability of linking only the precompiled and assembled standard library object modules to any C program. Taking the example under discussion (the program to print hello), the #INCLUDE preprocessor directive is deleted and the program is compiled, just like all the others discussed previously in this book. However, when the linking process is begun (following assembly), you simply link the minimum modules (PREF at the beginning and POST at the end for MS-DOS) and FORMATIO.OBJ with the C program itself. Obviously, it is nice to commit all these operations to a batch file so that only one command need be given for the entire operation, but the linking process takes place after compilation has been successfully completed and even after assembly. Using this method, only a few extra seconds are required for most applications.

An alternate method, for those who dislike giving up batch processing, is to make up several different batch files, which can be accessed to deliver different linkings. For example, batch file C.BAT would compile, assemble, and link all of the standard library modules to the C program. Batch file CF.BAT would accomplish basically the same thing, except only FORMATIO would be linked. These types of files would take up very little memory space, and enough of them could be accommodated in most situations to take care of any linking assignment.

Again, it should be understood that the standard library object files have C language counterparts in the SuperSoft C compiler package. The programs with the .C extension have not been compiled and are included on diskette, so they may be incorporated into C programs *before* the compiling process begins. The files with the same names, which include an OBJ extension, are simply there for your convenience, having been precompiled from the original C programs at the SuperSoft facility.

There are several other methods that may be used as alternatives to those outlined here. A recommended method for your compiler will probably be discussed in the documentation accompanying it. Because you may not be using the same compiler package chosen as the model for this book, you should understand that some compilers are fast while others are slow. A major trade-off in the design of any compiler involves the time required to compile a program, as opposed to the time required to execute it. Execution time is all-important for most applications, although a trade-off in compilation time, which it usually mandates, can be detrimental to people trying to learn to work in a new language. The SuperSoft C compiler package emphasizes speed of execution, so compilation speed is sacrificed to a degree. Other compilers may offer faster compilation time at the expense of execution. However, it is possible to speed up the time it takes to compile, assemble, and link a program so that it is in executable form. Some methods have been discussed in this chapter. Not much can be done from a user's standpoint to speed up execution. For this reason, speed of execution is all-important for the beginner as well as the seasoned pro, since the compiler must be versatile enough not to be quickly outgrown as the student progresses.

One other warning: While a specific C program that you write may include a function or functions found in only one or two library files, the files themselves may call for other files. Check your compiler manual to determine if this is done. If so, it will be necessary to link these additional files for a successful run. If you use the preprocessor directive in the program preamble, it is usually only necessary to include the file that contains the specific term or terms you have used in the program. If this file calls to another, the process will be automatically handled during the compilation process. It is only when linking object modules that you must be aware of one file's excursions into another.

Square Root

Figure 6-1 shows a simple program that will automatically return the square root of any number that is input. This program is designed more on an academic level than a practical one and uses getchar to read a character from

```
main()
{

      char x;

QRP:

      x=getchar();

      if(isalpha(x))
      {
      printf("\r");
      goto QRP;
      }

      int y;
      int z;

      y=x-'O';
      z=y*y;

      printf("\n");
      printf("THE SQUARE OF %d IS %d",y,z);
      printf("\n");

      goto QRP;
}
```

Figure 6-1   Program that Returns the Square Root of a Number.

the keyboard. Notice the isalpha macro in the if statement line. This tests for an alphabetical character rather than a numerical one. If the character is alphabetical, there is an automatic branch to QRP: and another character may be input.

It is necessary to go through a conversion, so variables y and z are set up as integers; y is equal to the value x minus the zero null-character extension. Variable z is then assigned the value of y squared (y*y). The three printf lines provide spacing and also print a message indicating the number that was input and the square root of that number. Incidentally, in most of these programs, I have attempted to simplify things by using separate printf lines for spacing purposes (to present a neat display). Other printf statements are used to display visible information on the screen. The center printf statement in this particular case prints the actual screen information, inserting decimal integers y and z at the proper points. The carriage return and line-feed characters can also be included at the beginning of any printf statement. This can cut down on the number of program lines and, thus, the overall size of the program.

When the first square root has been displayed, there is a branch to QRP: and you may input another value. Figure 6-2 shows an example of several program runs.

```
                            THE SQUARE OF 1 IS 1
                            2
                            THE SQUARE OF 2 IS 4
                            3
                            THE SQUARE OF 3 IS 9
                            4
                            THE SQUARE OF 4 IS 16
                            5
                            THE SQUARE OF 5 IS 25
                            6
                            THE SQUARE OF 6 IS 36
                            7
                            THE SQUARE OF 7 IS 49
                            8
                            THE SQUARE OF 8 IS 64
                            9
                            THE SQUARE OF 9 IS 81
```

Figure 6-2 Several Runs Using the Program of Figure 6-1.

Power Program

The program shown in Figure 6-3 goes one step further than the previous program. This one is used to raise a number, which is input via the keyboard, to a power. There are two character inputs here using getchar, and variables i and x are identified as characters at the opening of the program. Five other variables are assigned integer values. Following the identifier QRP:, the first printf line causes the screen to display the quoted prompt, which asks for the power to which the number is to be raised. This is assigned to the char variable i. The next series of printf lines place a space between the previous screen write and then print the value prompt on the screen, which asks for the number to be raised to the previous power. This number is assigned to the char variable x.

Integer variable ii is assigned a value equal to the integer value of char i minus 2. The reasons for this will be made known later. The integer variable xx is assigned the integer value of char x. The variable z is then equal to the value of xx squared.

It was fairly simple to get to this point, and regardless of what power is input to the program, the value is always squared at the beginning. At this point, a loop is entered. Integer variable y counts from 1 to the value of ii. It increments in steps of 1 ($++y$). Let's assume for the sake of discussion that we wish to raise 4 to a power of 2, or 4 squared. In this case, i is equal to 2 and x is equal to 4. In the conversion lines, ii will be equal to 2 minus the null character minus 2, so ii is equal to 0. Variable xx will be equal to 4, and variable z will be equal to 16 ($xx*xx$). Now, the loop is entered, and it begins counting at 1. However, ii is equal to 0, so our loop is really no loop at all. Therefore, the assignments within the braces are bypassed, and zz is equal to

```
main()
{
        char i;
        char x;
        int ii;
        int xx;
        int y;
        int z;
        int zz;

QRP:

        printf("RAISE TO WHAT POWER?\n");
        i=getchar();
        printf("\n");
        printf("WHAT VALUE?\n");
        x=getchar();
        printf("\n\n");

        ii=(i-'0')-2;
        xx=x-'0';
        z=xx*xx;

        for(y=1; y<=ii; ++y)
        {
          zz=xx*z;
          z=zz;
        }

        zz=z;

        printf("%d RAISED TO THE ",xx);
        ii=ii+2;
        printf("POWER OF ");
        printf("%d",ii);
        printf(" IS ");

        printf("%d\n\n",zz);
        printf("PRESS <ENTER> TO CONTINUE\n\n");

        getchar();
        goto QRP;
}
```

Figure 6-3   Program Used to Raise a Number to a Power.

the value of z. Recall that z is equal to xx squared. The next six lines print the value, the power to which it was raised, and the final answer on the screen, the answer being the value of zz. In this case, the prompt will be 4 RAISED TO THE POWER OF 2 IS 16. You can see that ii has been converted again by adding 2. This is used in one of the printf statements. However, instead of using printf("%d",ii);, it is just as easy to use putchar(i);, thus avoiding the need for converting ii again. Either way results in the same on-screen display.

Due to the nature of this program, the for loop is not really used unless a value is to be raised to a power of 3 or more. For the next example, let's assume that the value of 4 is to be raised to the power of 4. Here is what happens. The same variable assignments are made as before, except in this case, *ii* is equal to the integer 2 (4 minus 2). The variable *xx* is equal to 4. Again, *z* is equal to *xx* squared, or 16. Now, however, the loop is actually put to use. The variable *y* is assigned the value of 1 as a minimum and a maximum value of *ii,* which is now 2. Therefore, the loop will complete two passes. Within the loop, *zz* is assigned a value of *xx* (4) times *z* (16). The variable *z* is reassigned the value of 4 times 16, or 64. At this point, the value 4 has been cubed. But the loop has not timed out yet. It must complete one more pass. During the second pass, *zz* is assigned the value of *xx* (4) times *z* (now 64). The variable *z* is now equal to 256. The loop has completed its second pass and times out. The variable *zz* is now assigned the value of *z,* or 256, which is equivalent to 4 raised to the fourth power. The variable *zz* is then fed into the printf function lines, along with variables *xx* and *ii* described previously. Figure 6-4 shows a sample program run.

Day of the Week

Programs that calculate the day of the week based upon a calendar date are certainly nothing new to microcomputers. Many hundreds of different programs have addressed this subject alone. This is also the subject of the C program shown in Figure 6-5. This program will output the day of the week upon which any calendar date falls. You input the month, the day, and the year in three separate scanf functions. The scanf function is used here to read the keyboard and to make the various assignments. It would be possible to use a single scanf function line that would allow for the inputting of the month, day, and year as one series of numbers, but the longer method was chosen to make the program easier to understand.

There is a rather complex mathematical formula involved in determining on which of the seven days of the week a calendar day falls. In this program, the formula is spread over ten program lines and 11 integer variables are used in addition to the 3 integer variables assigned to the values of the month, date, and year. The first printf line below the QRP: identifier prompts you to input the month. This is handled as a number from 1 to 12. The scanf function immediately below this line reads this number from the keyboard. This function will allow up to 2 characters to be input. Therefore, if the month lies past September (10, 11, or 12), it is not necessary to press Enter. If it is an earlier month, it is necessary to press Enter (or any other nondigit key) to cause execution to continue. Remember, the scanf function is very similar to the INKEY$ function in BASIC, in that as soon as the required number of characters has been input, execution continues.

```
B>3
WHAT VALUE?
4

4 RAISED TO THE POWER OF 3 IS 64

PRESS <ENTER> TO CONTINUE


RAISE TO WHAT POWER?
2
WHAT VALUE?
5

5 RAISED TO THE POWER OF 2 IS 25

PRESS <ENTER> TO CONTINUE


RAISE TO WHAT POWER?
4
WHAT VALUE?
3

3 RAISED TO THE POWER OF 4 IS 81

PRESS <ENTER> TO CONTINUE


RAISE TO WHAT POWER?
5
WHAT VALUE?
4

4 RAISED TO THE POWER OF 5 IS 1024

PRESS <ENTER> TO CONTINUE


RAISE TO WHAT POWER?
5
WHAT VALUE?
6

6 RAISED TO THE POWER OF 5 IS 7776

PRESS <ENTER> TO CONTINUE
```

Figure 6-4 Program Run of Raised-Power Routine.

Two more prompts are provided asking for the input of the day of the month (1–31) and the year. The year is input in its entirety, as 1886 or 1901, for example. The next printf line simply adds line feeds for a neater screen display.

The actual formula itself is handled in the next ten lines. The formula itself is unimportant as far as this discussion is concerned, only that it has been input in standard form in C language. This formula involves integer mathematics and is therefore compatible with the SuperSoft C compiler (which does not support floating-point arithmetic).

The next program segment contains seven if statements, followed by

```
/*DAY OF WEEK CALCULATION*/

main()
{
      int m;
      int d;
      int y;

      int aa;
      int bb;
      int cc;
      int dd;
      int xc;
      int v1;
      int v2;
      int v3;
      int v4;
      int z;
      int zz;

QRP:

      printf("INPUT THE MONTH(1-12)\n");

      scanf("%2d",&m);

      printf("\n\n");
      printf("INPUT THE DAY(1-31)\n");

      scanf("%2d",&d);

      printf("\n\n");
      printf("INPUT THE YEAR\n");

      scanf("%4d",&y);

      printf("\n\n\n\n");

      aa=((6/10)+(1/m));
      bb=y-aa;
      cc=m+(12*aa);
      dd=bb/100;
      v1=dd/4;
      v2=dd;
      v3=((5*bb)/4);
      v4=(13*(cc+1)/5);
      z=v4+v3-v2+v1+d-1;
      zz=z-(7*(z/7))+1;

      {
        if(zz==1)
         printf("SUNDAY\n");
        if(zz==2)
         printf("MONDAY\n");
        if(zz==3)
         printf("TUESDAY\n");
        if(zz==4)
         printf("WEDNESDAY\n");
        if(zz==5)
         printf("THURSDAY\n");
```

Figure 6-5 Day-of-the-Week Program.

```
      if(zz==6)
       printf("FRIDAY\n");
      if(zz==7)
       printf("SATURDAY\n");
   }

      printf("\n\n\n");
      printf("PRESS <ENTER> TO INPUT NEW DATE.\n");

      getchar(xc);

      goto QRP;
   }
```

Figure 6-5 (Continued)

appropriate printf functions if the argument is true. The previous
mathematical formula worked in the program has assigned a value to integer
variable zz, which ranges from 1 to 7. The if statement lines test for the value
of zz and make the day-of-the-week assignments accordingly. If zz is equal
to 1, the day of the week is Sunday, and this appears on the screen. Following
the output of the correct day of the week, the user is prompted to press Enter
to input a new date. The getchar function is used to halt programming until
Enter is pressed, although any other key will do as well. However, when you
press Enter or the space bar, no character appears on the screen, which is
helpful for a less-congested display. At this point, there is a branch to the
identifier QRP: and the program is run again, allowing for the input of new
values. Figure 6-6 shows a sample program run for the date of December 27,
1938. As you can see, the day of the week was a Tuesday.

```
      INPUT THE MONTH(1-12)
      12

      INPUT THE DAY(1-31)
      27

      INPUT THE YEAR
      1938


      TUESDAY
```

Figure 6-6 Sample Program Run for the
Date of December 27, 1938.   PRESS <ENTER> TO INPUT NEW DATE.

Dice

If anyone had doubts at the beginning that this book about a system-level
language would be referenced as much as possible to equivalent functions
and statements in BASIC, this program should remove them completely.
The BASIC language, if remembered for only one thing, will probably be

known as the language in which more simulated dice games were written than any other. You may say that it is sacrilege to write such a program in C, but if it serves to provide even a slight bit of additional understanding in learning this language, then it is well worth the pages it consumes in this text.

The program shown in Figure 6-7 uses the equivalent of RANDOMIZE and RND in BASIC. These are new functions that were not discussed previously. The rest of the functions are pretty much standard. You may see something new, however. Certain lines have been added to the program to name it and identify some line functions. These are the equivalent of REM statements in BASIC. As you already know, these are nonexecutable statements inserted into programs to provide anyone who uses the line listing with a guide to its operation.

REM statements in C simply consist of an opening backslash followed by an asterisk, the remark, and the close, which consists of an asterisk and a backslash. These are not executed when encountered during the program run. They do tell you a bit about program operation, however.

```
        /* DICE GAME */
main()
{
      int p;
      int seed;
      int w;
      int x;
      int y;

      p=0;

      printf("PRESS ANY KEY.\n\n");

      seed=getchar();    /* SEED INPUT (ASCII) FROM KEYBOARD */

      srand(seed);       /* SEED VALUE INCORPORATED INTO SRAND */

      printf("\n\n\n\n");
QRP:
      x=(rand() % 6)+1;       /* FIRST RANDOM NUMBER (1 TO 6) */
      y=(rand() % 6)+1;       /* SECOND RANDOM NUMBER (1 TO 6) */

      printf("%d   %d",x,y);      /* DISPLAY OF RANDOM NUMBERS (x,y) */

      w=x+y;

      if(p>>0 && w==7 || p>>0 && w==11)
      {
       printf("\n\n");
       printf("%d   YOU LOSE!!\n",w);
       p=0;
       getchar();
       goto QRP;
      }

      if(p==w)
      {
```

Figure 6-7   Dice Program to Introduce srand and rand.

```
 printf("\n");
 printf("%d   IS A WINNER!!\n",w);
 p=0;
 getchar();
 goto QRP;
}

if(p>>0)
{
 printf("\n");
 printf("%d   IS YOUR POINT!! TRY AGAIN!!\n",p);
 getchar();
 goto QRP;
}

if(x==y)
{
 printf("\n");
 printf("DOUBLES\n");
}

if(x+y==2)
{
 printf("SNAKE EYES\n");
 printf("YOU LOSE!!\n");
}

if(x+y==12)
{
 printf("BOXCARS\n");
 printf("YOU LOSE!!\n");
}

if(x+y==7 !! x+y==11)
{
 printf("\n");
 printf("%d   A WINNER\n",w);
}

if(x+y!=7 && x+y!=11 && x+y!=2 && x+y!= 12)
{
 printf("\n");
 printf("%d   IS YOUR POINT\n",w);
 p=x+y;
}

getchar();
goto QRP;
```

Figure 6–7   (Continued)

In most versions of BASIC, the RANDOMIZE statement is used to reseed the random number generator. When RANDOMIZE is encountered, a prompt often appears on the screen, which instructs the operator to input any number to serve as a seed. The srand function in C performs similarly. The RND function in BASIC is replaced by the rand function in C.

Looking at the program, you will note that one of the variables is named seed. This is identified as an integer, as are the variables p, w, x, and y. The first printf line prompts the user to press any key. When this is done, the integer value of the key that was pressed is assigned to the variable seed.

The next line uses the srand function, along with seed, to reseed the random number generator. Another portion of the program is entered at this point; it assigns a random value of between 1 and 6 to variables x and y. These two lines are exactly identical to the BASIC equivalent of:

$$200 \quad X = INT(RND*6) + 1$$
$$210 \quad Y = INT(RND*6) + 1$$

The number returned to x and to y will always be an integer because these variables have been identified as integer types. In BASIC, it is necessary to use the INT function to accomplish the same thing.

The next printf line displays the values of x and y, and their sum is assigned to integer variable w. This game is set up to perform very much like the game of craps. It allows you to win with a roll of 7 or 11 on the first try, lose with box cars or snake eyes, or win by rolling your point without rolling a 7 or 11 in between. In this program, the variable p may be thought of as the point value. It is equal to more than 0 only when a 7, 11, 2, or 12 is not produced on the first roll.

The next line tests for the condition of w and p. Stated simply, it says if the value of p is more than 0 and the value of w is equal to 7, or the value of p is more than 0 and the value of w is 11, then execute the following function line. This if statement tests for a loss on the second or subsequent rolls. In such instances, p will be equal to the point value of the first roll. At this stage of the game, rolling a 7 or 11 constitutes a loss, and YOU LOSE is displayed on the screen. When this is done, variable p is reassigned the value of 0, and getchar is encountered to halt program execution temporarily until you hit a key. When this is done, there is a branch to QRP:.

Let's assume, however, that your point is 10 and you roll a 10 on the second attempt. The next if statement detects the condition of the second roll being equal to the point value contained in variable p. This invokes another prompt, which displays your second roll value followed by an announcement that you have won. As before, p is reassigned the value of 0, and there is a branch back to the beginning.

On a first roll, however, p will have a value of 0, so the third, fourth, fifth, sixth, seventh, and eighth if lines come into play. The second one in this series tests for the condition of x being equal to y. This means that doubles have been rolled, and this prompt is displayed on the screen. The next if statement checks for a loss, which occurs if x plus y is equal to 2 (snake eyes) or x plus y is equal to 12 (box cars). If neither of these conditions is true, other if statement lines test for the possibility of a win when x plus y is equal to 7 or 11. You will see logical OR and AND operators throughout these lines, which should be understood by now. The last if statement assigns a point value to variable p whenever the first roll produces a sum that is not 7, 11, 2, or 12. The third if statement line from the top reads the value of the next roll, and if it does not constitute a 7, 11, or the needed point value, it causes the machine to display your point, along with a prompt to try again. The program is far simpler to write that it is to explain, especially if you've written similar programs in BASIC.

Figure 6-8 shows a sample program run, where many different combinations have cropped up. While a craps game of this type is considered to be very simple and even infantile by many, it does demonstrate a few functions in C and as importantly, the similarities between C language statements and those found in BASIC.

```
3   5
8   IS YOUR POINT

5   2

7   YOU LOSE!!

5   1
6   IS YOUR POINT

2   4
6   IS A WINNER!!

2   3
5   IS YOUR POINT

4   4
5   IS YOUR POINT!! TRY AGAIN!!

3   4

7   YOU LOSE!!

4   3
7   A WINNER

2   1
3   IS YOUR POINT

6   5

11  YOU LOSE!!

2   1
3   IS YOUR POINT

6   4
3   IS YOUR POINT!! TRY AGAIN!!

2   2
3   IS YOUR POINT!! TRY AGAIN!!

5   5
3   IS YOUR POINT!! TRY AGAIN!!

3   4

7   YOU LOSE!!
```

Figure 6-8 Sample Run of Dice Program.

```
5   1
6   IS YOUR POINT

3   5
6   IS YOUR POINT!! TRY AGAIN!!

5   5
6   IS YOUR POINT!! TRY AGAIN!!

5   6
```

Figure 6-8 (Continued)   11   YOU LOSE!!

The atoi Function

A new function and an improved method of doing things is demonstrated by the program shown in Figure 6-9. This one is quite similar to a previous offering, which raised numbers to various powers. Whereas the previous program was restricted to single-digit inputs (using the getchar function), this one simplifies matters considerably by using the atoi function, which is used to converts a string of digits into its numerical equivalent. In other words, atoi converts the numerical content of a char value to an integer. This description may sound a bit familiar to a similar function in BASIC. In this latter language, the VAL function is used to extract the numerical equivalent of a string and convert it to a value, which is usually assigned to a numerical variable. The atoi function in C programming language is used in a like manner.

The program shown in Figure 6-9 uses the gets function to read the keyboard input. When the program is first run, the user is prompted to input the power and then the value. In both cases, gets is used to read the keyboard input. The char value i represents the power, while char value x is the value of the number to be raised to the power.

However, before these values can be used, it is necessary to convert them to integers. This is done using the atoi function. In the first line following the inputting of the value, the variable ii is assigned the integer value of atoi(i)-2. The variable xx is assigned the integer value of char x. This is the same method used in the previous power program to raise a value to any given power. From this point on, the program lines are very much identical to the previous program with one exception. There is no goto statement in this program. Yet, you may continue to input values as before. As a matter of fact, it is necessary to halt execution of the program manually or input -1 following the value prompt in order to have the machine stop execution on its own. While the goto statement is supported in the SuperSoft C compiler and in most other compilers as well, this statement is almost never used because it is not necessary. There are even a few compilers out at present that don't support goto because of this. While there may occasionally be a need

```
main()
{
        char i, x;
        int ii,xx,y,z,zz;

        while((atoi(x)) !=-1)
        {
        printf("RAISE TO WHAT POWER?\n");

        gets(i);

        printf("\n");
        printf("WHAT VALUE?\n");

        gets(x);

        printf("\n");

        ii=atoi(i)-2;
        xx=atoi(x);
        z=xx*xx;

        for(y=1; y<=ii; ++y)
        {
            zz=xx*z;
            z=zz;
        }

        zz=z;

        printf("%d RAISED TO THE ",xx);

        ii=ii+2;

        printf("POWER OF ");
        printf("%d", ii);
        printf(" IS ");
        printf("%d\n\n", zz);
        }
}
```

Figure 6-9 Program Demonstrating the atoi Function.

for this statement, in almost every instance, any program written with gotos and matching identifiers can be shortened and made more efficient by omitting them and committing the lines to be executed over and over again to a loop.

This is exactly what has been done in this program. The while statement near the beginning simply states that while the integer value of x is not equal to a value of -1, then continue to execute all the following lines. You can think of this program in other terms by imagining that the while statement line is replaced with an identifier such as QRP:. Also, following the last printf function in this program, there is a goto QRP;. This combination will give you exactly the same results, but it involves an additional program line. The method shown here is most often used, and again, you rarely see a goto statement in any C program.

The simple program shown in Figure 6-10 shows another power pro-

```
main()
{
        char i;
        int sq;
        int x;

QRP:

        gets(i);

        x=atoi(i);
        sq=x*x;

        printf("%d\n", sq);

        goto QRP;
}
```

Figure 6-10 Another Program That
Raises a Number to the Power of 2.

gram, which is used to square an input number. Here, we can see that goto
has been used so that the main portion of the program may be run over and
over again. Figure 6-11 shows the same program using a while loop. In all
other aspects, the program is exactly the same as that shown in Figure 6-10.
Only the identifier and goto statement have been removed.

```
main()
{
        char i;
        int sq;
        int x;

        while(atoi(gets(i)) !=0)
        {
        x=atoi(i);
        sq=x*x;

        printf("%d\n", sq);
        }
}
```

Figure 6-11 Program of Figure 6-10
Written Using a while Loop.

Armed with this knowledge, it should now be possible for you to go
back through the programs included at the front of this chapter and write
them in a different manner, one which does away completely with goto
statements.

Summary

The programs presented in this chapter have made use of some of the functions and statements that were discussed in detail earlier on in this book. A
few new functions have also been presented, and there are many more that
you will discover as you pursue this language further. It is hoped that this
book will serve as a starting point. In no way should it be assumed that the
functions, statements, and programs discussed here represent all this
language has to offer. As a matter of fact, these discussions have covered
only a small portion of this powerful language. There are many more func-

tions yet to be learned, especially in regard to file handling using C language. This subject is left for another book, but as we previously pointed out, files are handled using similar functions to those designed to read from the standard input and write to the standard output. C language is a very commonsense language, and these file handling functions are quite appropriately labeled. By knowing the purpose of the functions presented in this book, your transition to file programs should be quite easy. Most of the file functions have a standard input/output equivalent. This includes fprintf, fgets, fputs, and many other functions preceded by the letter f, which act upon files in the same way their standard input/output functions act upon the keyboard and the display screen.

If you wish to go much further with C language, you should certainly be on the lookout for the offerings of various software companies in this field. It is fervently hoped that, in the near future, an interpreter will be available in C. While many system-level programmers might look down on such an idea, the fact of the matter is that it's pretty hard to beat an interpreter when considering the educational aspects. With a C interpreter and any modern microcomputer, it would be possible to write short programs in C and run them immediately without waiting for a compiler to go through its passes. Certainly, an interpreter is slow, but only from an execution standpoint. When a student is learning a new language, numerous programming errors are always made. With an interpreter, the offensive line can be reconstructed and the program run immediately. Little changes such as this take only a second or two to correct, and the results can then be seen during the run. However, any mistake made in a program that is to be compiled means that after the correction is made, it will be necessary to go through the entire compilation process again. If many mistakes are made, this can mean hours of compilation time to arrive at a single successful program run, which may take less than 10 seconds.

By training with a good-quality C interpreter, many more students can progress much faster in C language. Certainly, when C has been mastered to a fair degree, the interpreter can be replaced with a good compiler, which is almost mandatory when the educational process has gone beyond the primary and intermediate stages. At this juncture, the speed offered by a compiled program is most important. Again, execution speed is best accomplished by a compiler. However, educational speed is probably best served by an interpreter.

Without a doubt, we are going to hear a lot more about C language as it makes its impact on the software and microcomputer industry. You've taken the first step in being a part of this new wave. You are learning the basics of this fascinating language. You must next move on to the intermediate steps and from such a springboard, who knows where you will end up?

7 GOING FURTHER WITH C

The main purpose of this book is to teach the basics of C in a manner that is easily grasped by anyone who has a minimum of 4 months or more operational experience with a microcomputer. Programming concepts are demonstrated through the presentation of actual programs and brief, simplistic descriptions rather than by discussing program operations on a machine level. In other words, if a certain function accomplishes a certain task, this text assumes that it is enough to know how to perform the task through C programming alone rather than go into detail about what that particular function does on the machine level.

Only a small portion of the C programming language has been discussed in these pages. There are many more functions at your disposal, which can be made to work for you in shortening programming time, as well as execution time. Only the very basics of using these terms has been explained. If you desire to continue your education in C programming language, no doubt you will discover the shortcuts that can be taken and maybe even invent a few tricks of your own.

If you have absorbed the information contained in the previous chapters, no doubt you are ready to begin to explore C language. You are still quite a long way from being an expert in this language, however. To reach this goal will require that you spend many, many more hours on the machine discovering the ins and outs of what you already know *and* that you consult other tutorial sources to broaden your education.

The present Bible of C language is *The C Programming Language,* by Brian W. Kernighan and Dennis M. Ritchie.* Other books from Bell Laboratories are offered through Prentice-Hall, Inc.; many of these are written at a higher level than the one you are studying at present. While these are excellent works, they are quite difficult reading for the rank beginner, who knows absolutely nothing about C language. An introductory book such as this one, however, can help pave the way for a better understanding of the advanced materials, which are becoming more and more abundant with each passing month.

It would appear that C is a language that is going to be with us for quite some time. I view it as a transitional language or, rather, one that has not seen a great deal of modification in the last 5 or 6 years, but which may be heavily modified in the near future due to the increasing popularity and more widespread use.

Today, it is quite easy to gain a sound education in BASIC because of its popularity and extremely widespread use. There are many, many books, programs, and tutorial guides available for this language on levels that can meet the needs of almost anyone. As of this writing, this is not true of C

---

*Brian W. Kernighan and Dennis M. Ritchie, *The C Programming Language* (Englewood Cliffs, N.J.: Prentice-Hall, Inc., 1978).

language, so if you're determined to move forward in this field, it will take far more effort than was probably the case during your "weaning" period in BASIC.

If you feel lost in all of this, you can rest assured that many other people are in the same category, some of whom know far more about the language than you do and who use it on a professional level. Only a few software houses are now offering C compilers, even though their programmers may have been using this language for many years. It is fair to say that those who have come out with C compilers have done so quite cautiously, in that it is difficult to predict where this language might go in regard to the personal computer market.

C language could become a mainstay among the mass markets associated with personal computer software, or it could remain in its present state as a valuable tool for the systems-level programmer. In both fields, C language is mandating change. Whether or not these mandates are strong enough or practical enough actually to effect an overall change in the operating habits of both types of individuals is yet to be seen.

In order to move forward with C programming language, I urge you to continue exploring its makeup by reading all materials that are available and just as importantly, by programming in C at every opportunity. While only a small portion of the standard library functions are discussed in this book, you will find that many of those not touched upon are similar to the ones discussed and can be learned quite easily from past experience. If you set a goal for yourself of becoming familiar with two new functions per week, you will have a working knowledge of the total library within a short period of time. Do not attempt to push on to a new function while an old one still contains highly relevant mysteries. This is not to say that each function must be completely mastered before moving on to another, as this will probably not be possible. The only way to understand most of what every function and statement has to offer in any language is to be familiar with the language as a whole. Unfortunately, the only way to learn a language as a whole is to study a grouping of functions and statements that basically describe the entire language. This step has been taken in the previous chapters in this book. When familiarity with the concept of C and the language as a single entity has been established, it is far easier to spread outward in all directions, taking in new functions as they are needed.

Quite probably, you may feel that you are well versed in BASIC, but there's a very good chance that even simple uses of an obscure statement or function are completely unknown to you. It is difficult to say to which functions or statements this may apply. The real answer will depend on your personal programming desires and operational habits. These probably include DEFUSR, VARPTR, WAIT, CDBL, among others. If you are familiar with these and have used them successfully, you are to be commended, although this may also indicate that your pursuits run to a specialized area of programming that requires these functions. You may be unfamiliar with other functions and statements, which another operator committed to memory long ago. In any event, it is a safe bet that no matter how long you've been programming in BASIC, you are not intimately familiar with every statement and function this language contains. Even if you are, there are bound to be many possible combinations and uses which you've never even dreamed of to this point.

You have a distinct advantage in learning any new language once you have mastered BASIC to a point where you feel comfortable programming in it. Since BASIC is probably the first language you ever learned, it must be assumed that you had nothing to go on prior to studying it. Now that you are attempting to learn C, it is not necessary to throw away what you've learned about programming in BASIC, but rather to bring it with you and make it work in a manner that will allow you to learn this and many other languages far more quickly.

There are disadvantages as well because, by learning BASIC, you have automatically developed preconceived notions about computer languages, many of which will not apply when studying C. Thankfully, however, many do. As the old saying goes, it's all in how you're brought up. If you were brought up with BASIC as your first language, all other languages will probably seem quite awkward, as well as strange and even nonsensical, upon first glance. To those who were brought up under assembler, PL, and others, BASIC is a bugaboo that defies all laws of programming structure.

When learning a new language, it is extremely easy to become frustrated. This may be especially true of C, since there are so few beginner-level texts available on this subject. Most of the texts I have seen thus far are really written for persons who are more familiar with FORTRAN, Pascal, and, certainly, assembler than with BASIC. This is understandable because most of the people writing about C have been brought up in a systems-level programming environment. In any event, while you may not find the going nearly as easy, your knowledge of BASIC may be enough to pull you through some of the more difficult reading and programming exercises, or at least you may know where to look (or whom to ask) to obtain the information you need. One phone call to the company that sold you your C compiler may be all that is necessary. I have found that in most instances, these companies are willing to answer questions and even let you know about recommended reading materials or other sources of information that you may find valuable. A few minutes of questions and answers with a pro in the field of C language may overcome the possibility of many hours, days, or even weeks of frustrating trial and error learning. This is not to say that trial-and-error learning is not valuable. It can be the most effective tutorial experience of all, and not just because of what you accomplish. It's what you don't accomplish, or what you accomplish that is undesirable, that can be the most beneficial.

The first rule in learning a new language is to keep an up-to-date diary. You may format it any way you wish, but it might be best to start by devoting a separate section to each of the functions found in C. Other sections might address identifiers, statements, operators, and so on. Any time you're trying to accomplish something in C and find that the result is different than expected, you might log this result, saving it for future reference. Of course, this does not apply to programs that contain errors causing a null program run, but simply combinations of statements and functions that bring about a potentially useful result, even though it's not the one for which you were programming. You might be surprised at what you can discover accidentally, which may lead to the furtherance of this education in a new language.

The second rule is to strike out into new areas of the language you are learning instead of sticking with the language elements that you have already mastered. This is a far easier habit to get into than it initially would seem to be. Once you learn to use a small number of functions and statements, the newer language elements that you have not yet mastered seem all the more difficult and frightening. If you're not careful, you may find yourself writing basically the same programs over and over again. I call this "playing," and while it is entertaining, this practice does little to further your education.

The third rule should be quite obvious. Therefore, it will probably be ignored and is stressed here. Don't concentrate too long or too hard on a problem. At such times, it might be wise to begin playing simply to get your mind off the immediate subject at hand. Better yet, get away from the machine entirely and allow your mind to rest before tackling this same problem again. There is nothing worse than programmer's fatigue to make a terribly difficult situation absolutely impossible.

The fourth rule is most important and is as simple as the previous one. Once you've worked out a problem successfully, enter it in your diary and also make a printer copy of the program, especially if it's long and complex. At the same time, include remarks about each important line in the program, either before compilation or on the printer copy form. There is nothing quite so distressing as working on a difficult programming problem into the wee hours of the morning, going to bed, and waking up the next morning to look at the same program, which now means absolutely nothing to you. Sure, it will be much easier to figure out what was accomplished by looking at the program, but a few simple remarks written at the moment the program was printed can save a lot of time.

The last rule is quite important and simply states that you should get someone else interested in this new language so that you both may study it simultaneously, helping each other along. From an earlier chapter, you learned that C language and the UNIX operating system were actually products of a small group of programmers, who were pushing each other along. Without this friendly competition and help, the two may never have come about. When two people are studying the same language, their different ways of approaching the same problem may combine to arrive at a suitable solution much faster. When two or more concepts are compared, this can breed other concepts, other ideas for exploring the new language.

As Brian Kernighan and Dennis Ritchie point out in their book, "*The C Programming Language*", it always helps to have a more knowledgeable programmer nearby to consult when a seemingly insurmountable problem crops up. This is not too tall an order when one is speaking of BASIC and most of the other well-known languages. However, persons who are knowledgeable in C language are not nearly so numerous and may even be impossible to find in your area. Here again is a situation where a phone call to the software company that provided your compiler can be of tremendous benefit. Personnel there may be able to help you directly, or they may advise you of the presence of an authority in your general area. In any event, it's worth a try.

As the popularity of C language among personal computer users continues to grow, it is to be hoped that there will be more and more literature that may be used for instructional purposes. At present, however, such materials are quite rare. Generally speaking, documentation provided with most compiler packages will not serve as direct teaching aids in the use of C. Most of these are written specifically to explain the use of the compiler itself and *not* how to program in C language. Most, however, do provide a quite thorough rundown on each of the functions that are supported, and these can effectively be used as reference sources.

I fully anticipate the announcement of an interpreter package, which addresses C language. When this is made available, it will be a sure sign that the software industry is anticipating tremendously increased popularity of C. This might even mean that the industry is trying to generate such popularity. With the advent of a good interpreter, C language will be available to thousands of additional users, who might not otherwise be inclined to go the compiler route. One would expect that documentation provided with the interpreter might be directed at teaching the use of the language itself. At this juncture, the rapid progression of many microcomputer enthusiasts into the world of C language will be unstoppable.

Persistence will pay off while educating yourself in C language. The information is out there. All you need do is ask the right questions of the right sources. No, it won't be easy, but if you keep at it, you will probably reach a level of proficiency in C language equivalent to that which you presently have in BASIC in a fractionally shorter period of time than it took you to reach this level with the latter. This, again, alludes to your present knowledge of

BASIC and the fact that this knowledge can speed education time in the new language field.

And there is quite a bonus to mastering C. This language is as different from BASIC as night and day in many operational aspects (although there are many similarities as well), but many other languages, such as PL/1 and FORTRAN, are not so far removed. If you're not familiar with these other languages, you may find that learning to program in them after gaining a good proficiency in C will be a relatively simple task.

C LANGUAGE
PRIMER APPENDICES

A Machine Configuration

The microcomputer configuration for writing and running programs in this book is described below. This is not a required configuration and is included only for your information abut the exact system used as a model in researching this book.

Microcomputer: IBM Personal Computer

CPU: Intel 8088

Memory: 128K Bytes

Disk Storage: 640K Bytes—Two 320K Byte Tandom $5\frac{1}{4}''$ Drives

Printer: IBM Dot Matrix (Identical to Epson MX-80 With Graftrax) 80 CPS

Monitor: Princeton Graphic Systems HX-12 High Resolution RGB Color

Operating System: MS-DOS

Compiler: SuperSoft C Compiler

Options: RS232 Asynchronous Communications Adapter (IBM) QuadBoard With 64K Memory Expansion, 1 Parallel and 1 Serial Port

Additional Software/Options: None

B Supersoft C Compiler Standard Library Functions

As I previously mentioned, the C compiler used as a model for researching this book was obtained from SuperSoft, Inc. in Champaign, Illinois. The majority of the standard library functions found in the original C language are also provided in the SuperSoft C source code and the rest in assembly code. The user discovers the details of implementation by examining that code.

This appendix discusses each of the library functions. It also tells you which library files contain each function. It should be understood that this discussion is based upon the implementation of these functions and externals by SuperSoft, Inc., although they will be identical or similar to the original applications, as determined by Bell Laboratories.

abs

The abs function is used to return the absolute value of i, or $-i$, if i is less than zero. This function is not available under MS-DOS or CP/M-86 because of an assembler keyword conflict.

Format:

int abs(i)

int i;

This function is found in the FUNC.C file.

absval

The absval function is used to return the absolute value of *i,* or *-i* if *i* is less than zero.

Format:

int absval(i)

int i;

This function is found in the FUNC.C file.

access

The access function is used to return TRUE (1) if the file is accessible to the given mode. Otherwise, it is FALSE (0).

Format:

BOOL access(filename,mode)

FILESPEC *filename;
unsigned mode;

alloc

The alloc function is used to allocate a contiguous memory region of length *n.* Every block it allocates starts on an even address. Its identical twin is malloc.

Format:

char *alloc(n)

unsigned n;

This function is found in the ALLOC.C file.

assert

The ASSERT function is used to print Assertion failed/n on the console. It exits if *b* is false. Otherwise, ASSERT merely returns.

Format:

BOOL ASSERT(b)
BOOL b;

This function is found in the CRUNT2.C file.

atoi

The atoi function is used to return the decimal integer value corresponding to the null-terminated ASCII string pointed to by *s*. If this string contains characters other than leading tabs, blanks, and a minus sign (all optional) followed by consecutive decimal digits, atoi returns 0.

Format:

int atoi(s)

char *s;

This function is found in the FUNC.C file.

bdos

The bdos function enables CP/M users to incorporate direct BDOS function calls into programs written in SuperSoft C. Programs utilizing bdos will not be portable beyond CP/M and the 8080 series CPU's. The bdos function sets machine register C to the value given in *c* and register pair DE to the value in *de* and initiates a bdos call. bdos expects register C to contain a valid bdos function number.

The bdos function returns a single byte (as an integer) identical to the contents of the A register, through which bdos returns its values. The value that bdos returns is not sign-extended.

Format:

int bdos(c,de)

int c, de;

This function is found in C2.RH, C2I86.RH, POST.ASM, MDEP.C, C2RT.ASM, or CCLAST.ASM, depending on which version of the compiler you have.

bios

The bios function is used to enable CP/M users to incorporate direct BIOS calls into programs written in SuperSoft C. Programs that call bios will not be portable beyond CP/M and the 8080 series CPU's. The bios function sets machine register pair BC to the value given in *bc* and register pair DE to the value given in *de* and initiates the appropriate bios call by transferring control to the BIOS jump vector entry point specified in jmpnum. This entry point may be specified numerically or symbolically.

The appropriate mnemonics or symbolic names for each entry point and the numerical value for each entry point are given below:

WBOOT	0	SELDSK	8
CONST	1	SETTRK	9
CONIN	2	SETSEC	10
CONOUT	3	SETDMA	11
LIST	4	READ	12
PUNCH	5	WRITE	13
READER	6	LISTST	14
HOME	7	SECTRAN	15

If jmpnum is either SELDSK (8) or SECTRAN (15), bios returns the value remaining in register HL after execution of the bios call. Otherwise, it returns the value remaining in register A, without sign-extension (that is, as a value between 0 and 255).

Format:

int bios(jmpnum,bc,de)

int jmpnum, bc, de;

This function is found in C2.RH and similar files.

brk

The brk function is used to set the external variable name CCEDATA to the memory byte pointed to by *p* and returns CCEDATA, which is equivalent to the pointer value it was passed. CCEDATA is initially set to the byte immediately following the last byte in your program's external data area. Since CCEDATA is used as a base value by the other dynamic memory-allocation functions, this properly initializes those functions for your program. You will almost never need to call brk in your own programs.

Format:

char *brk(p)

char *p;

This function is found in C2.RH and similar files.

ccall

The ccall function is used to set machine registers *hl, a, bc,* and *de* to the values given in *hl, a, bc,* and *de,* respectively, and calls the assembly language subroutine beginning at addr. The ccall function returns the value present in the *hl* register after execution of the subroutine. Programs calling ccall will not be portable beyond the 8080 series CPU's.

Format:

int ccall(addr,hl,a,bc,de)

char *addr, a;
int hl, bc, de;

This function is found in C2.RH and similar files.

ccalla

The ccalla function is identical to ccall, except that it is used to return the value present in the A register after execution of the subroutine. Programs calling ccalla will also not be portable beyond the 8080 series CPU's.

As an example of the use of this function, consider the following:

```
int bdos (c,de)
 char c;
 int de;
-{
         return ccalla(5,0,0,c,de);
 }-
```

The C function listed here is clearly an implementation of the function bdos in terms of ccalla. (This is not the way bdos is implemented.) Both ccall and ccalla may also be used to invoke assembly language subroutines of your own creation.

Format:

int ccalla(addr,hl,a,bc,de)

char *addr, a;
int hl, bc, de;

This function is found in C2.RH and similar files.

cconin

The cconin function is a physical console input and cannot be redirected.

Format:

char cconin( )

This function is found in C2.RH and similar files.

cconout

The cconout function is a physical console output and cannot be redirected.

Format:

cconout(c)

char c;

This function is found in C2.RH and similar files.

clearerr

The clearerr function sets the file error state to be clear.

Format:

clearerr( )

This function is found in the STDIO.C file.

com__len

The com__len function is used to return the length of the command line under CP/M only.

Format:

com__len( )

This function is found in C2.RH and similar files.

com__line

The com__line function is used to return the address of the command line under CP/M only.

Format:

com__line( )

This function is found in C2.RH and similar files.

close

The close function is used to close the file specified by the pointer fd to its file descriptor. The close function returns SUCCESS (0) if the file specified was successfully closed. The close function returns ERROR (−1) and does not close the file if: (1) fd does not point to a valid file descriptor; or (2) the file could not be closed due to an error at the operating system level.

The close function does not place an end-of-file (EOF) character in the buffer (if there is one associated with the file) and does not call fflush. If you call close for a file opened for buffered output via fopen without first calling fflush, you will lose any data remaining in that file's I/O buffer.

Format:

RESULT close(fd)

FILE *fd;

This function is found in the STDIO.C file.

codend

The codend function is used to return a pointer to the byte immediately following the end of the code for the root segment of your program. Unless you have reorigined your program's external data area, the value returned by codend will point to the beginning of that area. This function is not implemented in the SuperSoft C compiler as of this writing, but may be in future versions.

Format:

char *codend( )

cpmver

The cpmver function is used to return the value present in register HL after execution of a call to BDOS function 12. This return value, which is not sign-extended, is 0 if the calling program is running under CP/M versions released prior to Version 2.0, 0x0020 if it is running under CP/M Version 2.0, in the range of 0x0021 to 0x002F under versions subsequent to 2.0, and 0x0100 under MP/M. This function is useful in writing C programs to run under CP/M or MP/M, independent of version number. Programs calling cpmver will not be portable beyond CP/M and MP/M.

Format:

int cpmver( )

This function is found in the STDIO.C file.

creat

The creat function is used to create a file on disk with the file specification given in fspec and opens it for output. If the value of mode has the 0x80 bit set, then a readable-writable file is created. Otherwise, a read-only file is created. Any existing file with the same specification will be deleted.

The creat function, if successful, returns a pointer to a valid file descriptor for the file specified. You should store this pointer for subsequent use in your program. The creat function returns ERROR (−1) and does not create or open any file if: (1) not enough user memory is available to store a new file descriptor; (2) the file specification given is invalid; or (3) the file could not be created and opened due to an error at the operating system level.

Format:

FILE *creat(fspec,mode)

FILESPEC *fspec;
unsigned mode;

This function is found in the STDIO.C file.

endext

The endext function is used to return a pointer to the byte immediately following the last byte in your program's external data area. This value should be identical to the initial value of CCEDATA. This function is not currently implemented in the SuperSoft C compiler as of this writing.

Format:

char *endext( )

errno

The errno is not a function, but rather an external variable that will be set to an error code whenever an I/O error occurs. Note that it is not automatically cleared if no error occurs. There is no zero error message, so clearing errno is the accepted way to preset it for picking up error values. The perror function, which will be discussed later in this chapter, prints an error message on the console, given a nonzero error.

Format:

int ERRNO

evnbrk

The evnbrk function performs identically to sbrk, with the exception that it always returns an even value. The evnbrk function does this by skipping one byte if sbrk would return an odd value for the given n argument. The evnbrk function, if successful, returns a pointer to the first memory location in the block added. The evnbrk function returns a value of ERROR (-1) and adds no bytes to user memory if adding the number of bytes specified would: (1) overlap a stored program; (2) overlap the run-time stack; or (3) exceed the available memory. It is important to mention that calling evnbrk with a negative argument must not occur between calls to alloc.

Format:

char *evnbrk(n)

int n;

This function is found in the CRUNT2.C file.

exec

The exec function is used to perform an interprogram jump to the file specified in the null-terminated string pointed to by fspec. The exec function is a call to execl with two arguments: execl(fspec,0). It is included for compatibility with BDS C.

Format:

RESULT exec(fspec)

FILESPEC *fspec;

This function is found in the STDIO.C file.

execl

The execl function is used to perform an interprogram jump to the file specified in the null-terminated string pointed to by fspec. That is, it loads and executes the code that file fspec is assumed to contain. Interprogram jumping is sometimes referred to as *program chaining*. The execl function enables you to execute a series of programs successively with each program in the series overlaying the memory image of the preceding program.

Command line parameters may be passed to the invoked program in a series of null-terminated strings pointed to by arg1, arg2, ..., argn. The last argument (argn) must be zero. This is for compatibility with UNIX. Under CP/M, arg0 is ignored due to a feature of that operating system. The execl function constructs a command line from the strings pointed to by its arguments. (Under CP/M and MS-DOS, this means interleaving spaces between the arguments.)

Data may also be passed from the invoking program to the invoked program within files or through the external data area. To pass data within a file, the invoking program should close the file and the invoked program should reopen it. To pass data (including open file descriptors) through the external data area, the origin of that area must be the same for both programs. This can be accomplished by having both programs define the exact same set of globals.

The execl function returns ERROR (−1) because any return from execl is an error. This will happen if the file fspec does not exist or could not be read for any reason, preventing overlaying of the memory image of the invoking program and the execution of the invoked program. The invoked program can jump back to the invoking program via another call to execl.

This is a list function. It is found in the STDIO.C file.

Format:

RESULT execl(fspec,arg0,arg1,arg2,....,argn)

FILESPEC *fspec;
char *arg0, *argo, *arg2, ..., argn;

exit

The exit function is used to transfer control from program back to the operating system (causes an exit to the system level). The exit function never returns. It does not flush (write to disk) any output buffers or close any open files. The parameter *i* is currently ignored.

Format:

exit(i)

This function is found in C2.RH and similar files.

externs

The externs function is used to return a pointer to the first byte in the external data area of your program. Unless you have reoriginized this area, this value will be the same as that returned by codend. This function is not currently implemented in the SuperSoft C compiler as of this writing.

Format:

char *externs( )

fabort

The fabort function is used to free the file descriptor allocated to an open file without closing that file. The file is specified by the pointer fd to its file descriptor. Calling fabort will have no effect on the contents of a file opened for input only, but calling it for a file opened for output may cause the loss of some or all of the data written to that file. SuperSoft has included this function to allow for compatibility with BDS C, but does not recommend that it be used.

The fabort function, if successful, returns SUCCESS (0). It returns ERROR (−1) if fd does not point to a valid file descriptor.

Format:

RESULT fabort(fd)

FILE *fd;

This function is found in the STDIO.C file.

fclose

The fclose function is used to close a file opened for buffered output via fopen. The file is specified by the pointer fd to its file descriptor. The fclose function places an end-of-file (EOF) character at the current position in the file's I/O buffer and calls fflush before closing the file.

The fclose function returns SUCCESS (0) if the file specified was successfully closed. It returns ERROR (-1) and does not close the file if: (1) the file specified was not opened for buffered output via fopen; (2) fd does not point to a valid file descriptor; or (3) the file could not be closed due to an error at the operating system level.

Format:

RESULT fclose(fd)

FILE *fd;

This function is found in the STDIO.C file.

fflush

The fflush function is used to flush or write to file the current contents of the I/O buffer associated with a file opened for buffered output via fopen. The file is specified by the pointer fd to its file descriptor. The size of the I/O buffer is set when the file is opened. After a call to fflush, the file I/O pointer will point to just past the last byte accessed.

The fflush function returns SUCCESS (0) if the buffer was successfully written to file. (Calling fflush when the buffer is empty has no effect than to return SUCCESS.) The fflush function returns ERROR (-1) and does not flush the buffer if: (1) the file was not opened for buffered output via fopen; (2) fd does not point to a valid file descriptor; or (3) the entire contents of the buffer could not be written due to an error at the operating system level.

Format:

RESULT fflush(fd)

FILE *fd;

This function is found in the STDIO.C file.

fgets

The fgets function is used to read a maximum of $n - 1$ characters (bytes) from a file opened for buffered input via fopen into the string beginning at *s*. The file is specified by the pointer *fd* to its file descriptor. The fgets function will not read past a new line or more than $n - 1$ characters, whichever comes first. The fgets function then appends a null character to the characters read to create a null-terminated string.

The fgets function, if successful, returns a pointer to this string (identical to the value passed in *s*). The fgets function returns a null pointer value (0) if: (1) fd does not point to a valid file descriptor; (2) the file could not be read due to an error at the operating system level; or (3) the end of the file has been reached.

Format:

> char *fgets(s,n,fd)
>
> > char *s;
> > int n;
> > FILE *fd;

This function is found in the STDIO.C file.

fopen

The fopen function is used to create and/or open a file for buffered I/O with the file specification given in fspec. It uses open actually to open the file. Thus, full file specifications may be used. If fopen is successful, it returns a pointer to a valid file descriptor for the file specified. You should store this pointer for subsequent use in your program. The fopen function returns NULL (0) and does not create or open any file if: (1) the file mode is unrecognized; (2) not enough user memory is available for a new file descriptor; (3) the file specification given is invalid; or (4) the file cannot be opened or created due to an error at the operating system level.

For mode, you must specify one of the following: *w, a, r,* or *rw.* Which one you do specify determines the file's I/O mode, as indicated in the following:

w   write-only mode

a   write-only mode, append output to end of file

r   read-only mode

rw   read-write mode

If a file's I/O mode is either *w, a,* or *rw,* it is said to be *open for buffered output.* If a file's I/O mode is either *r* or *rw,* it is said to be *open for buffered input.*

The value you specify for buffer size determines the size of the I/O buffer associated with the file. This value is best set as a positive integral multiple of the system record size. (A system record is the minimum unit of data transferred during file I/O operations. Under CP/M, the system record size is 128 bytes. Under UNIX, this is 512 bytes.) A pointer to the first byte in this I/O buffer is stored in the file descriptor. Thus, only a point to this file descriptor need be passed to any of the other buffered file I/O functions.

Format:

FILE *fopen(fspec,mode,buffer__size)

    FILESPEC *fspec;
    char *mode;
    int buffer__size;

This function is found in the STDIO.C file.

fprintf

The fprintf function is identical to printf, except that instead of writing to the standard output, it writes its formatted output string to the I/O buffer associated with a file opened for buffered output via fopen, beginning at the current location in that buffer. Whenever that buffer becomes full, it is automatically flushed (that is, its entire contents are written to the file). The file is specified by the pointer fd to its file descriptor. The fprintf function is a list function.

The fprintf function returns SUCCESS (0) if its entire output string was successfully written to the buffer. However, due to the buffering of file I/O operations, such a return value cannot guarantee that this same string will be successfully written to the file because errors resulting from and affecting the outcome of a particular call to fprintf may not become apparent until some later function call causes that file's I/O buffer to be flushed. The fprintf function returns ERROR (−1) if: (1) fd does not point to a valid file descriptor; (2) the file was not opened for buffered output via fopen; (3) the file could not be written due to an error at the operating system level; or (4) the entire string could not be written to the file due to a lack of disk space.

Format:

RESULT fprintf(fd,format,arg1,arg2,...)

FILE *fd;
char *format;
...

This function is found in the FORMATIO.C file.

fputs

The fputs function is used to write the null-terminated string pointed to by s to the I/O buffer associated with a file opened for buffered output via fopen, beginning at the current location in that buffer. Whenever that buffer becomes full, it is automatically flushed (that is, its entire contents are written to the file). The file is specified by the pointer fd to its file descriptor. For each newline character ('/n') appearing in the string, a carriage return and a new line ("/r/n") are written to the buffer. The terminal null character is not written.

The fputs function returns ERROR (−1) and does not write the string if: (1) fd does not point to a valid file descriptor; (2) the file was not opened for buffered output via fopen; or (3) the file could not be written due to an error at the operating system level. Otherwise, fputs returns the number of bytes actually written to the buffer minus the number of carriage return characters inserted. However, due to the buffering of file I/O operations, such a return value does not guarantee that those same bytes will be successfully written to the file because errors resulting from and affecting the outcome of a particular call to fputs may not become apparent until some later function call causes that file's I/O buffer to be flushed.

Format:

RESULT fputs(s,fd)

char *s;
FILE *fd;

This function is found in the STDIO.C file.

free

The free function is used to free a block in memory previously allocated by a call to alloc. The argument *p,* which should be identical to the value returned by that call to alloc, is a pointer to the first memory location in the block. Allocated blocks may be freed in any order. To call free with an argument not previously obtained by a call to alloc is a serious error.

Format:

free(p)

char *p;

This function is found in the ALLOC.C file.

fscanf

The fscanf function is identical to scanf, except that the input string is read from the I/O buffer associated with a file opened for buffered input via fopen rather than from the standard input. The file is specified by the pointer fd to its file descriptor. The fscanf function begins reading at the current position in the I/O buffer. It stops reading when it has successfully assigned values to the bytes corresponding to each item listed in the format string or when it has reached the end of the file, whichever comes first. This is a list function.

If no errors occur, fscanf returns the number of values successfully assigned. It returns ERROR (-1) and performs no input if: (1) fd does not point to a valid file descriptor; (2) the file was not opened for buffered input via fopen; or (3) the file could not be read due to an error at the operating system level.

Format:

RESULT fscanf(fd,format,arg1,arg2,...)

FILE *fd;
char *format, *arg1, *arg2, ...;

This function is found in the FORMATIO.C file.

getc

The getc function is used to return one character (byte) as an integer (between 0 and 255, inclusively) in sequence from a file opened for buffered input via fopen. The file is specified by the pointer fd to its file descriptor. Carriage returns and line feeds are returned explicitly. The getc function returns ERROR (−1) if: (1) the file was not opened for buffered input; or (2) the end of the file has been reached.

Format:

int getc(fd)

FILE *fd;

This function is found in the STDIO.C file.

getchar

The getchar function is used to return the next character from standard input (the control device, such as the keyboard). If getchar encounters a Control-Z (CP/M's EOF marker), it returns a null character. If a program containing a call to getchar is running under CP/M and getchar encounters a Control-C, the program will be aborted and control will be returned to the routine that initiated that program.

Format:

char getchar( )

This function is found in the CRUNT2.C file.

gets

The gets function is used to read the next line from standard input (the control device, such as the keyboard) into the string beginning at *s*. The gets function replaces the newline character ('/n') or the carriage-return/newline combination ("/r/n") that terminates the input line with a null character to create a null-terminated string. Since gets does not test whether the string beginning at *s* is long enough to contain the input line, you should define this string so that it can contain the longest input line you could reasonably expect.

Format:

get(s)

char *s;

This function is found in the CRUNT2.C file.

getval

The getval function must be passed a pointer to a pointer to a null-terminated string of ASCII characters consisting of substrings separated by commas. Each substring should contain only leading blanks, tabs, or a minus sign (all optional), followed by consecutive decimal digits.

When getval is first called with a particular parameter satisfying the above requirements, it returns the decimal integer value corresponding to the first substring and increments the pointer pointed to by that parameter (the secondary pointer) so that it points to the first character in the next substring. Each subsequent call to getval with that same parameter returns the decimal integer value corresponding to the substring currently pointed to by the secondary pointer and increments that pointer so that.it points to the first character in the next substring.

Since getval returns a 16-bit signed binary integer, the value represented in any substring should not be greater than + 32,767 or less than −32,768.

If getval encounters an invalid character at the beginning of a substring, it returns a value of zero and increments the secondary pointer as before. If getval encounters an invalid character within a substring, it terminates the substring, returns the value corresponding to the valid characters read up to that point, and increments the secondary pointer as before. When getval encounters the terminal null character, it sets the secondary pointer to zero and returns a value of zero.

Format:

int getval(s)

char **s;

This function is found in the FUNC.C file.

getw

The getw function is used to return one integer in sequence from a file opened for buffered input via fopen. The file is specified by the pointer fd to its file descriptor. Carriage returns and linefeeds are returned explicitly. The getw function returns ERROR (−1) if: (1) the file was not opened for buffered input, or (2) the end of the file has been reached, or (3) if the integer equal to ERROR (−1) appears in the input file. Thus, errno should be checked for true error conditions. Calls to getc may be interspersed with calls to getw. There need not be any particular alignment of information in the input file.

Format:

int getw(fd)

FILE *fd;

This function is found in the STDIO.C file.

get2b

The get2b function is used to return a two-byte quantity from a buffered input stream. The get2b function is similar to getw and fread, except that it is invariant with respect to byte ordering.

Format:

int get2b(fd)

FILE *fd;

This function is found in the STDIO.C file.

index

The index function is used to return a pointer to the first occurrence of the character *c* in the string beginning at *s*. The index function returns a null pointer value (0) if c does not occur in the string.

Format:

char *index(s,c)

char *s, c;

This function is found in the FUNC.C file.

initb

The initb function is used to permit relatively convenient initialization of character arrays. It should be passed two parameters: the first, array, should be a pointer to an array or character; the second, *s,* should be a pointer to a null-terminated string of ASCII characters representing decimal integer values separated by commas. When called, initb converts each decimal integer value and assigns the least significant eight bits of that value to the corresponding element in the character array pointed to by the array.

If there are n integer values in the string and greater than n elements in the array, only the first n elements of the array will be assigned values and the contents of the remaining elements will be unaltered. If there are n integer values in the string and less than n elements in the array, bytes beyond the end of the array will be assigned values as if they were elements of the array and data may be overwritten in error. It is your responsibility to either prevent or provide for these situations.

Format:

initb(array,s)

char *array, *s;

This function is found in the FUNC.C file.

initw

The initw function is used to allow relatively convenient initialization of integer arrays. It should be passed two parameters: the first, array, should be a pointer to an array of integers; the second, *s,* should be a pointer to a null-terminated string of ASCII characters representing decimal integer values separated by commas. When called, initb converts each decimal integer value in the string beginning at *s,* in sequence, to a binary integer value and assigns that value to the corresponding element in the integer array pointed to by array.

If there are *n* integer values in the string and greater than *n* elements in the array, only the first *n* elements of the array will be assigned values and the contents of the remaining elements will be unaltered. If there are *n* integer values in the string and less than *n* elements in the array, bytes beyond the end of the array will be assigned values as if they were elements of the array and data may be overwritten in error. It is your responsibility to either prevent or provide for these situations.

Format:

初期 initw(array,s)

int *array;
char *s;

This function is found in the FUNC.C file.

inp

The inp function is used to return the value present at the input port designated in port after execution of an IN machine instruction for that port. This function is available only on machines for which the IN instruction or an equivalent is used.

Format:

int inp(port)

char port;

This function is available in C2.RH and similar files.

isalnum

The isalnum function is used to return true (1) if *c* is an ASCII alphanumeric character. Otherwise, it returns false (0).

Format:

BOOL isalnum(c)

char c;

This function is found in the FUNC.C file.

isalpha

The isalpha function is used to return true (1) if *c* is an ASCII alphabetical character. Otherwise, it returns false (0).

Format:

BOOL isalpha(c)

char c;

This function is found in the CRUNT2.C file.

isascii

The isascii function is used to return true (1) if *c* is an ASCII character. Otherwise, it returns false (0).

Format:

BOOL isascii(c)

char c;

This function is found in the FUNC.C file.

iscntrl

The iscntrl function is used to return true (1) if *c* is an ASCII control character. Otherwise, it returns false (0).

Format:

BOOL iscntrl(c)

char c;

This function is found in the FUNC.C file.

isdigit

The isdigit function is used to return true (1) if *c* is an ASCII character representing one of the decimal digits 0 through 9. Otherwise, it returns false (0).

Format:

BOOL isdigit(c)

char c;

This function is found in the CRUNT2.C file.

islower

The islower function is used to return true (1) if *c* is an ASCII lowercase alphabetical character. Otherwise, it returns false (0).

Format:

BOOL islower(c)

char c;

This function is found in the CRUNT2.C file.

isnumeric

The isnumeric function is used to return true (1) if *c* is an ASCII character representing a valid digit in the number system with the base specified in radix. Otherwise, it returns false (0). For example:

isnumeric('A',15)

returns true. The isnumeric function is defined only if $1 < radix < 36$.

Format:

BOOL isnumeric(c,radix)

char c;
int radix;

This function is found in the FUNC.C file.

isprint

The isprint function is used to return true (1) if *c* is a printable ASCII character. Otherwise, it returns false (0).

Format:

BOOL isprint(c)

char c;

This function is found in the FUNC.C file.

ispunct

The ispunct function is used to return true (1) if *c* is an ASCII character representing a punctuation mark. Otherwise, it returns false (0).

Format:

BOOL ispunct(c)

char c;

This function is found in the FUNC.C file.

isspace

The isspace function is used to return true (1) if *c* is an ASCII character representing a space, a tab, or a new line. Otherwise, it returns false (0).

(This function is included for compatibility with BDS C; the standard UNIX C function is iswhite.)

Format:

BOOL isspace(c)

char c;

This function is found in the FUNC.C file.

isupper

The isupper function is used to return true (1) if *c* is an ASCII uppercase alphabetical character. Otherwise, it returns false (0).

Format:

BOOL isupper(c)

char c;

This function is found in the CRUNT2.C file.

iswhite

The iswhite function is used to return true (1) if c is an ASCII character representing a space, a tab, a new line, or a formfeed. Otherwise, it returns false (0).

Format:

BOOL iswhite(c)

char c;

This function is found in the CRUNT2.C file.

isvalidf

The isvalidf function is used to return true (1) if fd is a valid file descriptor. Otherwise, it returns false (0).

Format:

BOOL isvalidf(fd)

FILE *fd;

kbhit

The kbhit function is used to test whether a character has been typed on the console keyboard, returning true if it has and false if it has not. More precisely, kbhit returns true (nonzero) if a character is present at the standard input (usually the keyboard). Otherwise, it returns false (0). This function is not available on systems that do not have such a function, such as UNIX.

Format:

BOOL kbhit( )

This function is found in the FUNC.C file.

lock

The lock function is used to lock a process in fast memory. It is a no-op under CP/M and MS/DOS.

Format:

lock( )

This function is found in the STDIO.C file.

longjmp

The longjmp function is used to restore the program state from the savearea. (savearea should be 6 bytes long on the 8080.) The program state includes all register variables, the return program counter, and the stack pointer, and savearea should have been previously used as an argument to setjmp. Upon a call to longjmp the same savearea, the state is restored, effectively appearing as if a return from setjmp has occurred, with the return value being *i*. The longjmp function is a generalized version of reset.

Format:

longjmp(savearea, i)

int i;
int savearea[];

The longjmp function is found in C2.RH and similar files.

malloc

The malloc function is used to allocate a contiguous memory region of length *n*. Every block it allocates starts on an even address.

The malloc function, if successful, returns a pointer to the first memory location in the block. You should store this pointer for subsequent use in your program. The malloc function returns a NULL pointer value (0) and does not allocate any memory if allocating a contiguous block of the size requested would overlap: (1) a stored program; (2) the run-time stack; or (3) a previously allocated block in memory.

Format:

char *malloc(n)

unsigned n;

This function is found in the ALLOC.C file.

movmem

The movmem function is used to copy the contents of the *n* contiguous bytes in memory beginning at source into the *n* contiguous bytes beginning at dest. There is no restriction on the overlapping of these two regions. The bytes in the region pointed to by source are unaltered unless they are over-written as a result of overlapping between the regions.

Format:

movmem(source,dest,n)

char *source, *dest;
int np

This function is found in the CRUNT2.C file.

nice

The nice function is used to set the priority of the current process. This is a null procedure under CP/M and MS/DOS.

Format:

nice(n)

int n;

This function is found in the STDIO.C file.

open

The open function is used to open the file specified in fspec for direct I/O. This file must already exist. The open function, if successful, returns a pointer to a valid file descriptor for the file specified. You should store this pointer for subsequent use in your program. The open function returns ER-ROR (−1) and does not open the file if: (1) not enough user memory is available for a new file descriptor; (2) the file specification given is invalid; (3) the file specified either does not exist or was not created via creat; or (4) the file could not be opened due to an error at the operating system level.

For mode, you must specify one of the following: 0, 1, or 2. Which one you do specify determines the file's I/O mode, as indicated in the following:

0   read-only mode
1   write-only mode
2   read-write mode

Format:

FILE *open(fspec,mode)

FILESPEC *fspec;
unsigned mode;

This function is found in the STDIO.C file.

otell

The otell function is used to return the byte offset, from the beginning of the currently accessed 512-byte block of a file, at which the next file I/O operation on that file will begin. The file is specified by the pointer fd to its file descriptor. The otell function does not indicate within which 512-byte block the I/O operation will begin.

Format:

unsigned int otell (fd)

FILE *fd;

This function is found in the STDIO.C file.

outp

The outp function is used to place the byte *b* at the output port designated in port and executes an OUT machine instruction for that port. This function is available only on machines for which the OUT instruction is used.

Format:

outp(port,b)

char port, b;

This function is found in C2.RH and similar files.

pause

The pause function is used to suspend execution of the calling program until a character is typed on the console keyboard. The pause function executes a null loop and tests whether input is present at the standard input (usually the console keyboard), exiting the loop and returning control to calling program only when it is. A character or characters must be read from the standard input before pause may return.

Format:

pause( )

This function is found in the FUNC.C file.

peek

The peek function is used to return the contents of the memory byte at addr. The function peek, which has been included for compatibility with BDS C, is redundant in C, since indirection is a feature of the language.

Format:

char peek (addr)

char *addr;

This function is found in the FUNC.C file.

perror

The perror function is used to print the string *s* and a colon; then perror prints a string interpreting the value of errno, the I/O error value. If errno is zero, no interpretation is printed.

Format:

perror(s)

char *s;

This function is found in the FUNC.C file.

pgetc

The pgetc function is identical to getc, except that it replaces the system end-of-line indicator with a '/n'. Under CP/M and MS-DOS, this means that whenever it encounters a carriage return character ('/r') followed immediately by a newline character ('/n'), it returns only the newline character. The pgetc function thus converts lines within files from CP/M to UNIX (ANSII) format.

Format:

int pgetc(fd)

FILE *fd;

This function is found in the STDIO.C file.

poke

The poke function is used to write the byte *b* into the memory byte at addr, where *b* must be an lvalue expression. The function peek, which has been included for compatibility with BDS C, is redundant in C, since indirection is a feature of the language.

Format:

poke(addr,b)

char *addr, b;

This function is found in the FUNC.C file.

pputc

The pputc function is identical to putc, except that it replaces the '/n' character with the system end of line character. Under CP/M and MS-DOS, this means that whenever it is passed a newline character ('/n'), it first writes a carriage-return character ('/r') to the file's I/O buffer and then writes the newline character it was passed. The pputc function thus converts lines written to files under UNIX (ANSII) to CP/M format.

Format:

int pputc(c,fd)

char c;
FILE *fd;

This function is found in the STDIO.C file.

printf

The printf function is used to write a formatted output string to the standard output (usually the console screen). The printf function must be passed the pointer, format, to a null-terminated string. (A string constant is also valid for format because it evaluates to a null-terminated string.) This string controls the generation of the output string. The printf function may be passed a series of other arguments: arg1, arg2, ... The individual arguments in this series may be characters, integers, unsigned integers, or string pointers. Only the first argument, format, is required; all others are optional. This is a list function.

The string pointed to by format may contain either ordinary characters or special substrings, beginning with the character %, that are called *conversion specifications*. Each ordinary character, when encountered by printf as it scans the string from right to left, is simply written to the standard output. Each conversion specification, when encountered, causes the value of the next argument in the series arg1, arg2, ... to be converted and formatted as specified and written to the standard output.

Following the character % in each conversion specification, there may appear:

1. An optional minus sign, '−', which, if present, causes the converted value to be left-adjusted in its field. Right-adjustment is the default.

2. An optional string of decimal digits specifying the minimum number of characters in the field in which the value is to be written. The converted value will never be truncated. However, if it has fewer characters than are here specified, it will be padded on the left (or right if left-adjustment has been specified) with spaces to the width specified. If this digit string begins with a zero, the converted value will be padded with zeros instead of spaces.

3. Another optional string of decimal digits, which must be preceded by a period, '.', specifying the maximum number of characters to be copied from a null-terminated string.

4. A character, called the conversion character, indicating the type of conversion to be performed.

Of the above, only the conversion character must be present in a conversion specification. All the others, if present, must be in the order they are listed.

The (valid) conversion characters and the types of conversions they specify are:

c The least significant byte of the argument is interpreted as a character. That character is written only if it is printable.

d The argument, which should be an integer, is converted to decimal notation.

o The argument, which should be an integer, is converted to octal notation.

x The argument, which should be an integer, is converted to hexadecimal notation.

u   The argument, which should be an unsigned integer, is converted to decimal notation.

s   The argument is interpreted as a string pointer. Characters from the string pointed to are read and written until either a null character is read or an optionally specified maximum number of characters has been written. See (3) in the list above.

%   The character % is written. This is an escape sequence. No argument is involved.

Format:

                    printf(format,arg1,arg2,...)

                         char *format;
                              ...

This function is found in the FORMATIO.C file.

putc

The putc function is used to write the character *c* to the I/O buffer associated with a file opened for buffered output via fopen, beginning at the current location in that buffer. Whenever that buffer becomes full, it is automatically flushed (that is, its entire contents are written to the file). The file is specified by the pointer fd to its file descriptor.

The putc function returns ERROR (−1) and does not write the character if: (1) fd does not point to a valid file descriptor; (2) the file was not opened for buffered output via fopen; or (3) the buffer could not be written due to an error at the operating system level. Otherwise, putc writes the character to the file's I/O buffer and returns SUCCESS (0). However, due to the buffering of file I/O operations, such a return value does not guarantee that that same character will be successfully written to the file because errors resulting from and affecting the outcome of a particular call to putc may not become apparent until some later function call causes that file's I/O buffer to be flushed.

Format:

                       int putc(c,fd)

                          char c;
                          FILE *fd;

This function is found in the STDIO.C file.

putchar

The putchar function is used to write the character *c* to the standard output (usually the console screen).

Format:

putchar(c)

char c;

This function is found in the CRUNT2.C file.

puts

The puts function is used to write the string beginning at *s* to the standard output (usually the console screen). All carriage commands must appear explicitly in this string.

Format:

puts(s)

char *s;

This function is found in the CRUNT2.C file.

putw

The putw function is used to write the integer *i* to the I/O buffer associated with a file opened for buffered output via fopen, beginning at the current location in that buffer. Whenever that buffer becomes full, it is automatically flushed (that is, its entire contents are written to the file). The file is specified by the pointer fd to its file descriptor.

The putw function returns ERROR (−1) and does not write the integer if: (1) fd does not point to a valid file descriptor; (2) the file was not opened for buffered output via fopen; or (3) the buffer could not be written due to an error at the operating system level. Otherwise, putw writes the integer to the file's I/O buffer and returns SUCCESS (0). However, due to the buffering of file I/O operations, such a return value does not guarantee that that same integer will be successfully written to the file, since errors resulting from and affecting the outcome of a particular call to putc may not become apparent until some later function call causes that file's I/O buffer to be flushed. Calls to putc and putw may be interspersed. Files written with putc and putw may be read using getc and getw.

Format:

RESULT putw(i,fd)

int i;
FILE *fd;

This function is found in the STDIO.C file.

put2b

The put2b function is used to output a two-byte quantity to a buffered output stream. The put2b function is similar to putw and fwrite, except that it is invariant with respect to byte ordering.

Format:

int put2b(i, fd)

int i;
FILE *fd;

This function is found in the STDIO.C file.

rand

The rand function is used to return the next value in a pseudorandom number sequence initialized by a prior call to srand. Values in the sequence will range from 0 to 65,535.

The C expression

rand( ) % n

will evaluate to an integer greater than or equal to 0 but less than *n*.

Format:

int rand( )

This function is found in the FUNC.C file.

read

The read function is used to read a maximum of *n* bytes from a file
opened for either direct or buffered input, beginning at the current location
of the file I/O pointer, into the memory buffer pointed to by bufr. The file is
specified by the pointer fd to its file descriptor. You should define the buffer
pointed to by bufr such that it can contain at least *n* bytes.

The file I/O pointer will always point to the beginning of a system
record. After a call to read, the file I/O pointer will point to the beginning of
the system record following the last one read.

If no errors occur, read returns the actual number of bytes read. If
those bytes are being read from a file, read returns either a multiple of the
system record size or zero (0). Zero will be returned only if the end of the file
has been reached. If bytes are being read from a serial device opened as a file,
read returns one (1), since only one byte per call to read can be read from a
serial device. The read function returns ERROR (−1) and does not attempt
to read the file if: (1) the file was not opened for input; (2) *n* is less than the
system record size; or (3) the file could not be read due to an error at the
operating system level.

Format:

int read(fd,bufr,n)

FILE *fd;
char *bufr;
int n;

This function is found in the STDIO.C file.

realloc

The realloc function is used to change the size of the allocated region
pointed to by *p* (*p* must have been previously set by a call to malloc). The
realloc function preserves the content of the region, as best can be done,

since the region may have a new size. The realloc function returns a pointer to the new size region.

Format:

char *realloc(p,nbytes)

char *p;
unsigned nbytes;

This function is found in the ALLOC.C file.

rename

The rename function is used to rename the file specified in fspec, giving it the name contained in the null-terminated string pointed to by fname. (A string constant, such as newname, is also valid for fname, since it evaluates to a pointer to a null-terminated string.) The drive name and the number, if any, are unchanged.

Format:

RESULT rename(fname,fspec)

char *fname;
FILESPEC *fspec;

This function is found in the STDIO.C file.

reset

The reset function is used to cause program execution to return to the point set by a prior call to setexit. This transfer has the appearance of a return from setexit. The parameter *n* passed to reset appears as the value returned by setexit.

The reset and setexit functions together allow simpler and cleaner coding of repeated exits to a common point, particularly when such transfers require unraveling a number of levels of function calls. For example, in writing an interactive editor, you could call setexit at the top of the command loop and test whether or not its apparent return value was equal to zero. Each nonzero value could be used to indicate a different error condition. The error number could be printed and command loop execution could continue.

Calls to reset would be sprinkled in appropriate places throughout the loop. In each instance, the parameter passed to reset would indicate the presence (nonzero) or absence (zero) of a particular error condition.

The reset and setexit functions, while they resemble functions in usage and syntax, are implemented as compiler preprocessor directives rather than as functions. Thus, you will not find them in any of the standard library function files.

Format:

reset(n)

int n;

rindex

The rindex function is used to return a pointer to the last occurrence of the character *c* in the string beginning at *s*. The index function returns a null pointer value (0) if c does not occur in the string.

Format:

char *rindex(s,c)

char *s, c;

This function is found in the FUNC.C file.

rtell

The rtell function is used to return the offset, in 512-block bytes, from the beginning of a file of the 512-byte file block within which the next file I/O operation on that file will begin. The rtell function does not indicate the offset into that block at which the I/O operation will begin. The file is specified by the pointer fd to its file descriptor.

Format:

unsigned int rtell(fd)

FILE *fd;

This function is found in the STDIO.C file.

sbrk

The sbrk function is used to add *n* bytes to user memory (increments CCEDATA by *n*). The sbrk function, if successful, returns a pointer to the first byte in the block added. The sbrk function returns a value of ERROR (−1) and adds no bytes to user memory if a block of the size specified would: (1) overlap a stored program; (2) overlap the runtime stack; or (3) exceed the available memory. It is important to note that calling sbrk with a negative argument must not occur between calls to alloc.

Format:

char *sbrk(n)

int n;

This function is found in the CRUNT2.C file.

scanf

The scanf function is used to read a formatted input string from the standard input (usually the console keyboard). Under control of the format string pointed to by its first argument, format, scanf extracts a series of substrings, known as *input fields,* from its input string, converts the values represented in each of these fields, known as *input values,* and assigns these converted values in sequence to the objects pointed to by its remaining arguments arg1, arg2, ... This is a list function.

As its first argument, scanf must be passed a pointer, format, to an appropriate null-terminated string. (A string constant is also valid for format, since it evaluates to a pointer to a null-terminated string.) A series of other arguments, arg1, arg2, ..., may be passed to scanf, all of which must be pointers. The individual objects pointed to by arg1, arg2, ..., may be either characters, character arrays, or integers.

The format string may contain either white-space characters (that is, spaces, tabs, and newlines), ordinary characters, or special substrings, beginning with the character %, known as *conversion specifications.* The first conversion specification in the format string corresponds to and determines the boundaries of the first input field in the input string. It also determines the type of conversion to be performed on the input value represented in that field. Each successive pair of conversion specifications and input fields bears this same relationship.

Following the character % in each conversion specification, there may appear:

1. An optional assignment suppression character, '*', which, if present, causes the corresponding input field to be skipped.
2. An optional string of decimal digits specifying the maximum number of characters in the corresponding input field.
3. A character, called the conversion character, indicating the type of conversion to be performed on the corresponding input value.

Of the above, only the conversion character must be present in a conversion specification. All the others, if present, must be in the order they are listed above.

The valid conversion characters and the types of conversions they specify are:

%   A single % character is expected in the input string at this point. This is an escape sequence; no assignment is performed.

c   The input value is interpreted as a character. The corresponding argument should be a character pointer. The normal skip over space characters is suppressed. To read the next nonspace character, use %ls. If a field width is also specified, the corresponding argument should be a pointer to an array of characters, and the specified number of characters will be read.

s   The input value is interpreted as a character string. The corresponding argument should be a pointer to an array of characters large enough to hold the string in addition to a terminal null-character added by scanf. The input field is terminated either by a space or a new line, or when the maximum number of characters has been read, whichever comes first.

[The input value is interpreted as a character string. The corresponding argument should be a pointer to a character array large enough to hold the string plus a terminal null-character added by scanf. Where the input field is terminated is determined as follows. The left bracket is followed by a set of characters and a right bracket. If the first character in that set is not a circumflex, '^', the input field is terminated by the first character not in the set within the brackets. If the first character is a circumflex, the input field is terminated by the first character in the set within the brackets (the '^' excluded).

d   The input value is interpreted as a decimal integer and is converted to a binary integer. The corresponding argument should be an integer pointer.

o   The input value is interpreted as an octal integer and converted to a binary integer. The corresponding argument should be an integer pointer.

x The input value is interpreted as a hexadecimal integer and is converted to a binary integer. The corresponding argument should be an integer pointer.

The central task of scanf is to determine the boundaries of the input fields in its input string, which contain the input values to be converted and assigned. To find these substrings, scanf scans the characters in its input string, comparing each of them with the corresponding characters in the string pointed to by format. If a character in the input string matches the corresponding character in the format string, it is discarded and the next character in the input string is read. If the corresponding characters do not match, scanf returns immediately. Note that any amount of white space in the input string matches any amount of white space in the format string. White space in the format string is optional (it is ignored), while, in the input string, it can delimit input fields. Thus, corresponding characters are not simply those characters that are the same number of bytes from the beginning of their respective strings. Whenever the character %, which introduces a conversion specification, is encountered in the format string, the corresponding character in the input string is assumed to be the first byte of an input field. An input field extends either until a space character is encountered in the input string or the number of bytes specified for the field width has been read, whichever comes first. The conversion characters c and [discussed earlier are the only exceptions to this otherwise general rule. Any inappropriate character in an input field causes scanf to return immediately.

The scanf function returns either the number of converted input values it assigned or, if no input is present at the standard input, the constant EOF.

Format:

RESULT scanf(format,arg1,arg2,...)

char *format;

...

This function is found in the FORMATIO.C file.

seek

The seek function is used to set the value of the file I/O pointer associated with an open file. The file is specified by the pointer fd to its file descriptor and may have been opened for either direct or buffered I/O. The seek function is used primarily in conjunction with tell and the direct file I/O functions read and write. The seek function must be used with more care in conjunction with the buffered file I/O functions in order to prevent data loss.

The value assigned to offset has a different interpretation depending on the value assigned to origin:

If origin is 0, then the file I/O pointer will point to the beginning of the file plus offset bytes.

If origin is 1, then the file I/O pointer will point to its current position in the file plus offset bytes.

If origin is 2, then the file I/O pointer will point to the end of the file plus offset bytes.

If origin is 3, then the file I/O pointer will point to the beginning of the file plus offset times 512 bytes.

If the origin is 4, then the file I/O pointer will point to its current position in the file plus offset times 512 bytes.

If origin is 5, then the file I/O pointer will point to the end of the file plus offset times 512 bytes.

Format:

int seek(fd,offset,origin)

FILE *fd;
int offset;
int origin;

This function is found in the STDIO.C file.

setexit

The setexit function is used to set its location as the reset point, the point to which subsequent calls to reset transfer program execution. Each call to reset that follows causes an apparent return from the function setexit. The setexit function appears to return the value of the parameter *n* that was passed to reset.

Format:

int setexit( )

This function is found in C2.RH, and so on.

setjmp

The setjmp function is used to store the program state in the savearea. (savearea should be 6 bytes long on the 8080.) The program state includes all register variables, the return program counter, and the stack pointer. It then returns 0. Upon a call to longjmp with the same savearea, the state is restored, effectively appearing as if a return from setjmp has occurred, with the return value being supplied by longjmp. The setjmp function is a generalized version of setexit.

Format:

setjmp(savearea)

int savearea[];

This function is found in C2.RH and other files.

setmem

The setmem function is used to set the n contiguous bytes beginning at p to the value specified in b. You can use setmem to initialize a variety of buffers and arrays.

Format:

setmem(p,n,b)

char *p;
int n;
char b;

This function is found in the CRUNT2.C file.

sleep

The sleep function is used to suspend execution for n tenths of a second on a Z80 CPU running at 4 MHz. You can tailor this function to a different CPU and/or block rate by changing the value of one or two constants.

Format:

sleep(n)

unsigned n;

This function is found in the FUNC.C file.

sprintf

The sprintf function is identical to printf, except that it writes its formatted output into the string beginning at *s*. Contrast this with printf, which writes its output to the standard output, and fprintf, which writes its output to a file. The sprintf function appends a null character to the formatted output string. This is a list function.

Format:

sprintf(s,format,arg1,arg2,...)

char *s, *format;

...

This function is found in the FORMATIO.C file.

srand

The srand function is used to initialize the return value of rand to the value passed in seed.

Format:

srand(seed)

int seed;

This function is found in the FUNC.C file.

sscanf

The sscanf function is identical to scanf (and fscanf), except that its formatted input string is read from the null-terminated string beginning at s rather than from the standard input. The sscanf function does not read the terminal null character. This is a list function.

Format:

sscanf(s,format,arg1,arg2,...)

char *s, *format, *arg1, *arg2, ...;

This function is found in the FORMATIO.C file.

strcat

The strcat function is used to append a copy of the string beginning at s2 to the end of the string beginning at s1, creating a single null-terminated string. Note that the resulting string begins at s1 and contains a single, terminal null character.

The strcat function returns a pointer to the resulting string, identical to the parameter s1 that it was passed.

Format:

char *strcat(s1,s2)

char *s1, *s2;

This function is found in the FUNC.C file.

strcmp

The strcmp function is used to compare the string beginning at s1 with the string beginning at s2. This comparison is similar to an alphabetical comparison, except that it is based on the numerical values of corresponding characters in the two strings. This comparison ends when the first null character in either string is encountered.

The strcmp function returns a positive integer, zero (0), or a negative integer depending on whether the string beginning at s1 is greater than, equal to, or less than the string beginning at s2, respectively.

Format:

$$\text{int strcmp(s1,s2)}$$

$$\text{char *s1, *s2;}$$

This function is found in the FUNC.C file.

strcpy

The strcpy is used to copy the string beginning at *s2* into the string beginning at *s1*, stopping after a null character has been copied. If the length of the string beginning at *s2* is greater than the length of the string beginning at *s1*, data in the bytes following the latter may be overwritten in error.

Format:

$$\text{strcpy(s1,s2)}$$

$$\text{char *s1, *s2;}$$

This function is found in the FUNC.C file.

streq

The streq function is used to compare the first *n* characters in the strings beginning at *s1* and *s2*, where *n* is the number of characters (excluding the terminal null) in the string beginning at *s2*. The streq function returns n if the corresponding characters in the two strings are identical; otherwise, it returns zero (0).

Format:

$$\text{int *streq(s1,s2)}$$

$$\text{char *s1, *s2;}$$

This function is found in C2.RH, among others.

strlen

The strlen function is used to return the number of characters (excluding the terminal null) in the string beginning at *s*.

Format:

int strlen(s)

char *s;

This function is found in the CRUNT2.C file.

strncat

The strncat function is identical to strcat, except that strncat appends at most *n* characters from the string beginning at *s*2 (truncating from the right) to the end of the string beginning at *s*1.

Format:

char *strncat(s1,s2,n)

char *s1, *s2;
int n;

This function is found in the FUNC.C file.

strncpy

The strncpy function is identical to strcpy, except that strncpy copies exactly *n* characters into the string beginning at *s*1, truncating or null-padding the string beginning at *s*2 if necessary. The resulting string may not be null-terminated if the string beginning at *s*2 contains *n* or more characters.

Format:

char *strncpy(s1,s2,n)

char *s1, *s2;
int n;

This function is found in the FUNC.C file.

swab

The swab function is used to copy *n* bytes from *s*1 to *s*2, swapping every pair of bytes.

Format:

swab(s1,s2,n)

char *s1, *s2;
int n;

This function is found in the STDIO.C file.

tell

The tell function is used to return the byte offset from the beginning of a file at which the next I/O operation on that file will begin. The file is specified by the pointer fd to its file descriptor. If tell is called for a file greater than 64K long, its return value is subject to arithmetic overflow.

Format:

unsigned int tell(fd)

FILE *fd;

This function is found in the STDIO.C file.

tolower

The tolower function is used to return the lowercase equivalent of *c* if *c* is an uppercase alphabetical ASCII character. Otherwise, it returns *c*.

Format:

char tolower(c)

char c;

This function is found in the FUNC.C file.

topofmem

The topofmem function is used to return CCEDATA.

Format:

char *topofmem( )

toupper

The toupper function is used to return to uppercase equivalent of *c* if *c* is a lowercase alphabetical ASCII character. Otherwise, it returns *c*.

Format:

char toupper(c)

char c;

This function is found in the CRUNT2.C file.

ungetc

The ungetc function is used to write the character *c* into the most recently read byte of the I/O buffer associated with a file opened for buffered input via fopen. The ungetc function also decrements the pointer to the next byte to be read from the file I/O buffer so that it points to the byte that was just written.

The ungetc function, if successful, returns an undefined value. It returns ERROR (-1) if it could not perform its function (for instance, if the file specified was not opened for buffered input via fopen).

To call ungetc for a file serves no purpose unless one of fgets, fscanf, getc, or getw (the buffered file input functions) has been previously called for the same file. Only one call to ungetc between calls to the buffered file input functions for a given file can be guaranteed to have the desired effect.

Format:

RESULT ungets(c,fd)

char c;
FILE *fd;

This function is found in the STDIO.C file.

ugetchar

The ugetchar function is used to cause the next call to getchar to return
c. Calling ugetchar more than once between successive calls to getchar will
have no effect on the state of the standard input.

Format:

ugetchar(c)

char c;

This function is found in the CRUNT2.C file.

unlink

The unlink function is used to delete the file specified in fspec from the
file system. The unlink function returns SUCCESS (0) if the file was successfully deleted. It returns ERROR (−1) and does not delete the file if: (1)
the file specification given is invalid; or (2) the file could not be deleted due to
an error at the operating system level.

Format:

RESULT unlink(fspec)

FILESPEC *fspec;

This function is found in the STDIO.C file.

wait

The wait function is used to block the execution of the process until the
completion of the process with process id pid. The wait function returns ER-
ROR (−1) if no such process id is waiting. It always returns immediately with
an ERROR value under CP/M-80 and MS-DOS.

Format:

RESULT wait(pid)

unsigned pid;

This function is found in the STDIO.C file.

write

The write function is used to output the number of bytes specified in num_bytes from the area pointed to by buffer. Output is to a file opened for direct (unbuffered) output. The file is specified by a file descriptor, *fd*.

The write function returns the actual number of bytes written. This may be less than num_bytes. If the file descriptor is invalid or the file cannot be read, a value of ERROR (−1) is returned to indicate an error.

Every file descriptor contains a pointer to the next record to be accessed in file I/O operations. A call to write advances that pointer by the number of bytes written. A subsequent call to read or to write will begin at the new position of this pointer. By calling seek, you may alter the position of this file I/O pointer without reading or writing.

Format:

```
int write (fd,buffer,num_bytes)

FILE *fd;
char *buffer;
int num_bytes;
```

This function is found in the STDIO.C file.

xmain

The xmain function is the first C function called upon program startup. It sets up the arguments to main, does I/O redirection if the switch REDIRECT is set in CUSTOMIZ.H before CRUNT2.C is recompiled. I/O redirection is the ability to redirect the console input, the console output, or command arguments to be from files. Console input is redirected by specifying a file name preceded by a ' < ' on the command line. Console input is then taken from the file. Console output is redirected by specifying a file name preceded by a ' > ' on the command line. Console output is then sent to that file. Command argument redirection is specified by preceding a file name with a ' ' on the command line. Command arguments are then taken from the file.

Command-line arguments are passed to the program by setting up two parameters in the call to main. The left parameter is the count of the number of arguments. The right parameter is an array of pointers to strings, one string for each argument.

If the command line and I/O redirection code is not desired, or if a different action is required, a program can be specified with its top-level procedure being xmain rather than main.

Format:

xmain( )

This function is found in the CRUNT2.C file.

xrev

The xrev function is used to reverse the array of values pointed to by &nargs[1]. The count of pointers is assumed to be in nargs[0]. This procedure is used to rework the parameters in list functions.

Format:

xrev(nargs)

int *nargs;

This function is found in the FORMATIO.C file.

xrprintf

The xrprintf function does all the work for printf and others. It expects an area (line) to write its output string and an array of arguments (args). The first element of args should be a format string.

Format:

xrprintf(line,args)

char *line;
int *args;

This function is found in the FORMATIO.C file.

xrscanf

The xrscanf function does all the work for scanf et al. Xrscanf expects to be passed two functions: kind(where) should return a byte from the input and u__kind(c,where) should push back a byte into the intput. Format is a pointer to the format string and args is the array of addresses to the variables to be set by the input. Because xrscanf makes use of a global static for some interfunction communication, it cannot be called recursively.

Format:

xrscanf(kind,u__kind, where, format, args)

    int (*kind) (), (*u__kind) (), where;
    int *args;

This function is found in the FORMATIO.C file.

C   Supersoft C Compiler Standard Library Functions and Externals

Standard Library Functions and Externals

ALLOC.C

alloc	free	malloc	calloc
realloc			

C2.RH, C2I86.RH, POST.ASM, MDEP.C, C2RT.ASM, or CCLAST.ASM

bdos	bios	brk	ccall
ccalla	exit	inp	longjmp
outp	reset	setexit	setjmp
streq	cconin	cconout	com__len
com__line	errno		

CRUNT2.C

evnbrk	getchar	gets	isalpha
isdigit	islower	isupper	iswhite
movmem	putchar	puts	sbrk
setmem	strlen	toupper	ubrk
assert	ugetchar	wrdbrk	xmain

FUNC.C

abs	absval	atoi	perror
getval	index	initb	initw
isalnum	isascii	iscntrl	isnumeric
isprint	ispunct	isspace	kbhit
min	max	pause	peek
poke	putdec	qsort	rand
rindex	sleep	srand	strcat
strcmp	strcpy	strncat	strncmp
strncpy	substr	tolower	isdecimal

STDIO.C

close	cmpver	creat	exec
execl	fabort	fclose	fflush

fgets	fopen	fputs	fread
fwrite	getc	getw	isserial
link	open	otell	pgetc
pputc	putc	putw	read
rename	rtell	seek	tell
ungetc	unlink	write	wait
lock	nice	swab	isatty
isserial	clearerr	freopen	fdopen
isvalidf	ferror	fileno	fgetc
fputc	get2b	put2b	

FORMATIO.C

fprintf	fscanf	printf	scanf
sprintf	sscanf	xrprintf	xrscanf
xrev			

D C Language Keywords

Keywords are used as identifiers in C language and may not be used for other purposes, such as variable names.

auto	goto
break	if
case	int
char	long
continue	register
default	return
do	sizeof
double	struct
else	switch
entry	typedef
extern	union
float	unsigned
for	while

E C Language Statements

break	goto
case	if
continue	if else

default   return
do   while   switch
for   while

F   Preprocessor Directives

define   identifier token-string
define   identifier(identifier , ... , identifier) token-string
else
endif
if   constant-expression
ifdef   identifier
include   "filename"
include   < filename >
line   constant identifier
undef   identifier

G   C Language Declarations

abstract-declarator:

empty
(abstract-declarator)
* abstract-declarator
abstract-declarator ()
abstract-declarator [constant-expression$_{opt}$]

declaration:

decl-specifiers init-declarator-list$_{opt}$;

deci-specifiers:
type-specifier decl-specifiers$_{opt}$
sc-specifier decl-specifiers$_{opt}$

declarator:

identifier
(declarator)

* declarator

declarator ()

declarator [constant-expression$_{opt}$]

init-declarator:

declarator initializer$_{opt}$

init-declarator-list:

init-declarator

init-declarator , init-declarator-list

initializer:

= expression

= { initializer-list }

= { initializer-list , }

initializer-list:

expression

initializer-list , initializer-list

{ initializer-list }

sc-specifier:

auto

extern

register

static

typedef

struct-decl-list:

struct-declaration

struct-declaration struct-decl-list

struct-declaration:

type-specifier struct-declarator-list ;

struct-declarator:

    declarator

    declarator : constant-expression

    : constant-expression

struct-declarator-list:

    struct-declarator

    struct-declarator , struct-declarator-list

struct-or-union-specifier:

    struct { struct-decl-list }

    struct identifier { struct-decl-list }

    struct identifier

    union { struct-decl-list }

    union identifier { struct-decl-list }

    union identifier

typedef-name:

    identifier

type-specifier:

    char

    double

    float

    int

    long

    short

    unsigned

    struct-or-union-specifier

    typedef-name

H   C Language Expressions

expression:

    primary

    * expression

& expression
− expression
! expression
   expression
+ + 1value
− − 1value
1value + +
1value − −
sizeof expression
(type-name) expression
expression binop expression
expression ? expression : expression
lvalue asgnop expression
expression, expressiong

1value:

identifier
primary [expression]
1value . identifier
primary → identifier
* expression
(1value)

primary:

identifier
constant
string
(expression)
primary (expression-list$_{opt}$)
primary [expression]
1value . identifier
primary → identifier

INDEX